JOHN
AND THE
JESUS BOAT
EPISODE TWO

ROLIN
BRUNO

AD 28 WOES AND COMFORT

STONEWALL PRESS
PAVING YOUR WAY TO SUCCESS

Copyright © 2018 by Rolin Bruno.

Cover credits to: Yigal Allon Center, Ginosar, Israel, and the Israel Antiquities Authority

Episode number two in the series, John and the Jesus Boat

Originally published as JOHN!, Library of Congress 2015916378.

All rights reserved. No part of this book may be used or reproduced by any means, graphic, electronic, or mechanical, including photocopying, recording, taping, or by any information storage retrieval system without the written permission of the author except in the case of brief quotations within critical articles or reviews.

Scripture quotations taken from the New American Standard Bible, Copyright 1960, 1962, 1963, 1968, 1971, 1972, 1973, 1975, 1977, 1995 by The Lockman Foundation. Used by permission. (www. Lockman.org)

Scripture taken from the Holy Bible, NEW INTERNATIONAL VERSION. Copyright 1973, 1978, 1984, 2011 by Biblica, Inc. All rights reserved worldwide. Used by permission.

NEW INTERNATIONAL VERSION and NIV are registered trademarks of Biblica, Inca. Use of either trademark for the offering of goods or services requires the prior written consent of Biblica US, Inc.

Scripture quotations taken from The Holy Bible, English Standard Version (ESV), copyright 2001 by Crossway, a publishing ministry of Good News Publishers. Used by permission. All rights reserved.

Scripture taken from Good News Translation (Today's English Version, Second Edition) copyright 1992 American Bible Society.

Scripture quotations taken from the Holy Bible, New Living Translation, copyright 1996, 2004. Used by permission of Tyndale House Publishers, Inc., Wheaton Illinois 60189. All rights reserved.

Printed in the United States of America

ISBN: 978-1-64460-050-4 (Paperback)
ISBN: 978-1-64460-049-8 (eBook)

Library of Congress Control Number: 2018964494

 STONEWALL PRESS
PAVING YOUR WAY TO SUCCESS

Stonewall Press
363 Paladium Court
Owings Mills, MD 21117
www.stonewallpress.com
1-888-334-0980

About the Cover

The Storm on the Sea of Galilee (1633) by Rembrandt van Rijn, master painter from the Dutch Golden Age.

The Story

The Storm tells a tale from the Bible (Mark 4:35, Luke 8:22). Jesus told his disciples, "Let's go over to the other side of the lake." But a fierce storm arose and the boat was in danger. Jesus was asleep on a cushion, so his disciples woke him, saying, "Teacher, don't you care that we are dying?"

The Boat

1600 years later, Rembrandt set out to paint the scene. He made some good guesses for what the boat looked like, portraying it barely large enough to carry thirteen people, But he would not have known it had four rowing positions and a flat bottom which made it hard to manage in high winds.

The Discoveries

In 1986, one of these boats was found buried in a muddy Galilee beach, and became known as "the Jesus Boat." Previously, a tile mosaic (below) was found in nearby Magdala showing how similar boats of the age appeared.

The Painting

This work passed in and out of private hands until it came to rest in the Gardner Museum of Boston. But in 1990 the museum was breached, and priceless paintings were stolen, including *The Storm*. It has not been seen since, and there is a ten million dollar reward on offer for its return.

About the Author

Rolin Bruno is a Bible scholar and street evangelist with a vivid imagination that fills the gaps in Bible stories.

He has served as pastor at a storefront church on Skid Row in Los Angeles and as a street evangelist in the cities of Southern California, Western Pennsylvania, and the Gulf Coast of Mississippi.

Rolin has a calling to serve the homeless. In Louisiana and Mississippi, he served as a home missionary to stricken residents after the devastation of Hurricane Katrina, teaching spiritual disciplines and twelve-step recovery from addictions. In Pennsylvania, he served as a street evangelist to pre-teen street kids, and helped lead them through the Youth Alpha program to answer their questions about God and Jesus.

Rolin is a 2003 BA graduate of Vanguard University of Southern California, studying religion and ministry. He continued at Vanguard to earn a Master's degree in religion and Bible. His 2006 master's thesis is on the letter of Jude, "Jude and the Scoffers." This 278-page opus is available for purchase at http://www.tren.com.

He is an ordained deacon of the Communion of Evangelical Episcopal Churches and of the Anglican Communion in North America, and has a heart for planting new Celebrate Recovery chapters.

Rolin lives in the mountains of Southern California and is an avid camper and backpacker. He has hiked the Grand Canyon, Mount Whitney, the Inyo Mountains, and 570 miles of the Pacific Crest Trail.

Contents

About the Author: v
Prologue: Stop, Thief! xi
        Friday 16 April AD 28, 5:30 pm

1:    Lord of the Sabbath 1
        Saturday 17 April AD 28, 8:00 am

2:    Trumpets and Charity 3
        Tuesday 20 April AD 28, 9:00 am

3:    Bethesda Pools 9
        Saturday 24 April AD 28, 11:00 am

4:    Adultery Forgiven 13
        Sunday 25 April AD 28, 6:00 am

5:    Son of God 15
        Monday 26 April AD 28, 4:30 am

6:    Another Passover 21
        Wednesday 28 April AD 28, 11:00 am

7:    The Withered Hand 25
        Saturday 1 May AD 28, 8:00 am

8:    Escape 27
        Sunday 2 May AD 28, 4:00 am

9:    Roadies 29
        Thursday 6 May AD 28, 4:00 pm

10:	Groupies 31
	Sunday 9 May AD 28, 7:00 am
11:	Jesus and the Twelve 37
	Monday 10 May AD 28, 5:00 am
12:	Rock Star 41
	Tuesday 11 May AD 28, 8:00 am
13:	Mary of Magdala 45
	Wednesday 12 May AD 28, 5:00 pm
14:	The Centurion's Servant 47
	Sunday 29 May AD 28, 10:00 am
15:	Chuza the Syrian 49
	Monday 30 May AD 28, 2:00 pm
16:	Pray for Your Enemies 55
	Tuesday 1 June AD 28, 6:00 am
17:	Who You Gonna Call? 57
	Thursday 3 June AD 28, 10:00 am
18:	On the Road Again 61
	Tuesday 15 June AD 28, 2:00 pm
19:	Woes and Comfort 65
	Friday 18 June AD 28, 4:00 pm
20:	Message to the Baptist 69
	Friday 2 July AD 28, 2:00 pm
21:	A Woman Anointing 73
	Thursday 8 July AD 28, 7:00 am
22:	The Witch of Endor 77
	Wednesday 21 July AD 28, 10:00 am
23:	Back to the Lake 81
	Sunday 25 July AD 28, 2:00 pm

24:	Parable instead of a sign 87
	Monday 26 July AD 28, 5:00 am
25:	Weeds and Nets 95
	Tuesday 27 July AD 28, 10:00 am
26:	Seeds and Leaven 99
	Tuesday 10 August AD 28, 10:00 am
27:	Scripture and Feasting 103
	Wednesday 18 August AD 28, 12:00 noon
28:	Treasure and Light 107
	Thursday 9 September AD 28, 10:00 am
29:	Cost of Discipleship 109
	Thursday 30 September AD 28, 4:00 am
30:	Storms and Demons 115
	Friday 1 October AD 28, 2:00 am
31:	Personae Non Gratae 123
	Wednesday 6 October AD 28, 4:00 pm
32:	Twelve Years 125
	Thursday 7 October AD 28, 12:00 noon
33:	You Can't Go Home 129
	Friday 5 November AD 28, 4:00 pm
34:	Hometown Humbling 133
	Saturday 6 November AD 28, 10:00 am
35:	Parting of the Ways 137
	Sunday 5 December AD 28, 12:00 noon
36:	Six Roads 143
	Monday 6 December AD 28, 8:00 am
37:	Emmaus 147
	Thursday 9 December AD 28, 1:00 pm

38: Twelve Tales 151
    Wednesday 5 January AD 29, 4:00 pm

Epilogue: Dance of Death 157
    Wednesday 5 January AD 29, 7:00 pm

Notes and Suggested Bible Readings: 161

Prologue

Stop, Thief!

FRIDAY 16 APRIL AD 28, 5:30 PM

"Stop, you thieves! Get out of my garden!"

John and Andrew were startled, and looked up from what they were doing.

It was just after sunset, the beginning of Sabbath, and they had fallen behind Jesus and his disciples, who were walking far ahead. They had stopped to pick some cucumbers and small melons from the vines growing across the path. They were also picking heads of grain from the edge of the grainfield, then rubbing them in their hands to shred off the chaff, and eating them, for they were hungry.[1]

A small boy had been watching them, and then run off. Now the boy was back, along with two angry men. The boy picked up some stones and began to throw them at John and Andrew, and the men started to follow suit.

"Run, John!" said Andrew, and he took off, with John at his heels. The men ran after them a few yards and then dropped off. John and Andrew ran ahead until they found a fig tree that could hide them.

Andrew collapsed into the deep shade of the tree, gasping and laughing. "Oh, that was fun! I guess we showed them who was faster, didn't we? The last time I got chased out of a farmer's field I was eleven years old and hanging with Philip."

John was breathless and exhilarated, but he was angry. He said, "They had no right to chase us away. Moses' law says a farmer has to leave behind what grows along the path and at the edges of the field. That's set aside for the poor and for travelers like us!" [2]

"Well, I guess not everyone follows the Law, John, even this close to Jerusalem."

"Yeah, you're right," John said. "But if Judas Kerioth had bought us all some food when we were passing Jericho, we wouldn't have been so hungry. He sure is stingy with the money."

Andrew said, "Yeah, he complains a lot about expenses. But I wonder if he's siphoning off some of the money for himself."

"Wow," John said, "maybe we should watch him closer."

"Yeah," Andrew said. "Hey, why did Jesus leave the main road and take this side path?"

"I think we're taking a shortcut over to Gibeah to make it to the evening synagogue service," said John. "From there it's only three miles south to Jerusalem."

"Well, I've caught my breath now. Let's run and catch up to Jesus and the rest. We don't wanna be late for synagogue—if it's crowded we might end up standing outside the door."

"Good point. And I have a few of those little melons I can share with the others."

"Me too. They're yummy."

1

LORD OF THE SABBATH

SATURDAY 17 APRIL AD 28, 8:00 AM

John and Andrew followed Jesus into the synagogue for the morning service. They were early, for Jesus wanted to watch the people arrive. He had been asked to read and speak in today's service. Last night the two teens had stood at the back of the evening service, and John had seen the boy who threw rocks at them standing with one of the men who chased them. They had noticed John, but avoided looking at him.

After the evening service, Jesus and the twenty disciples traveling with him had gone to an upper room in Gibeah where a splendid meal was waiting for them, including some scrumptious barbecued goat. John and Andrew had eaten their fill, while feeling guilty about thinking that Judas of Kerioth was stingy or dishonest in his guardianship of the money purse. They slept that night with full bellies.

But Jesus seemed to know something was bothering them.

The people of Gibeah were beginning to arrive at the synagogue, along with disciples Peter, Philip, Thomas, and John's big brother James. Two men dressed as Pharisees came in the door, followed by the man and his son from the previous day's farmyard chase. They ignored John and Andrew, but the Pharisees approached Jesus, while the man and his son stood by and watched.

One of the Pharisees said, "Teacher, we have been told that your disciples were gathering heads of grain from a field on the Sabbath, and then they were rubbing them in their hands so they could eat them. Moses tells us that all food preparation must be done before Sabbath begins. Why do your disciples do what is unlawful on the Sabbath?"

Jesus had a twinkle in his eye. He said, "Haven't you read what David did before he took his throne, when he and his companions were hungry? David went into the house of God, took the consecrated bread, and ate what is lawful only for priests to eat. He also gave some to his companions." [3]

The Pharisees scowled. "Would you then make yourself equal to King David?"

In a more serious tone, Jesus said, "The Sabbath was made for man, not man for the Sabbath. So the *Son of Man* is Lord even over the Sabbath." [4]

They scowled even more, and stepped outside to discuss it among themselves.

When they had gone, Jesus said to John and Andrew, "Tell me, young men, did your hunger lead you into sin, or not?"

They both started to talk at once. Then Andrew continued, "Yes, teacher, it did. We were thinking bad things about Judas of Kerioth because he didn't buy food for us. We were very wrong." John nodded in agreement.

Jesus said to them, "Strive be masters of your appetites, so no one will take advantage of you. But I tell you the truth: the day is coming when you will eat of the body of the *Son of Man*, and drink of his blood."

John and Andrew were startled, but didn't have the nerve to ask Jesus what he meant by that.

2

TRUMPETS AND CHARITY

TUESDAY 20 APRIL AD 28, 9:00 AM

"Hezzy! Come out!"

Hezekiah's face appeared at the doorway of the mud hut. "John!" he yelled. "Hey, glad you're here! Did Jesus come with you?" At ten years old, he was taller than the last time John had seen him, and the tunic he was wearing was conspicuously too short for him.

"Yes he did," John said, "and he's got a chore for you. Can you come out?"

"Oh, yes! Just a minute." He disappeared into the house to talk to his mother and then bounced exuberantly back out the door. He said, "Where's Jesus?"

John said, "He's waiting for us at the Synagogue of David. Come on! Let's run!"

They were there in a flash, and bounded up the steps and inside to where Jesus was talking with Rabbi Yanai. Peter and Big James were listening.

"Ah, there you are, Hezekiah," said Jesus. "I have a task for you. Rabbi Yanai has been telling me of several men and women who are unable to leave their homes but have asked to see me." Jesus smiled and said, "Today, Doctor Jesus will be making house calls."

Hezekiah was to be their tour guide. The Rabbi told him about each person they were going to visit. Hezekiah knew where most of them lived, and got directions for the ones unknown to him. He led Jesus and his crew off through the narrow, twisty maze of little streets and back alleys that made up the City of David, Jerusalem's slum zone.

Arriving at a humble mud hut, Simon Peter and James kept watch outside while Jesus and the two youngsters went in. An elderly blind man was living there alone, with no family to help him. "Lord Jesus," he said, "I am honored to meet you. I heard about you, and tried to get to the synagogue the last time you were speaking there. But I took a wrong turn and ended up sleeping in the street that night. Someone finally recognized me and guided me back home."

Jesus asked him, "Do you believe I can help you?"

"Yes, Master, I do. My neighbors bring me food, but I need someone who can come once or twice a week and guide me to places far off, like the synagogue."

Jesus placed his hands on the man's head. "Joshua son of Matthiel, close your eyes." The old man did so. "Now open them and see," Jesus commanded.

The man complied, and then exclaimed, "Oh my Lord, I see you! I see! I see!"

"Tell no one of this," said Jesus. "And go give thanks to God in the temple."

From there they continued to six more dwellings, several of them humble, and some quite livable and comfortable. Jesus healed some who were lame, some who were sick and feeble, and an infant who was burning up with fever.

The last house was where a playmate of Hezekiah lived. Jesus went inside with Hezekiah while Peter, James, and John stood outside talking. Peter said to James, "If you and I are going to be bodyguards for Jesus, we should probably be carrying swords. I heard that some of the Pharisees and temple chiefs are suggesting that somebody should kill Jesus."

John said, "When I was with Jesus at the temple last year, the captain of the temple guard drew his sword and threatened Jesus with it. Jesus just walked away from him."

James said, "Simon, I think you're right. Jesus is in danger. My father has two swords in Bethsaida. When we get home I'll ask him for the short one. I can hide it under my clothes."

"I have a short sword at my house, too," said Peter. "I'll carry it next time we leave home."

By mid-afternoon, Peter, James, and John were relaxing just inside the synagogue while Jesus was talking with the rabbi. He was telling Jesus what the Pharisees' association had done after their embarrassment last year. They had arranged for fifty lambs to be sold in the City of David at discount prices, two weeks before this year's Passover.

Rabbi Yanai had helped the families of the district band together in groups to buy lambs, so that every family would be able to participate in Passover. However, the lambs had not been inspected by the priests, and the families had to pay the inspection fees. Several of the lambs had blemishes and could not be used for the temple sacrifice, but the families sold those and rearranged the sharing of the unblemished lambs. No one would be left out this year.

Suddenly Hezekiah rushed in from outside shouting, "There's a parade coming! I hear trumpets!"

Peter, James, and John went outside to look, and sure enough, coming down the street were three horses mounted by flag bearers, led by three servants blowing trumpets. These were followed by three more horses mounted by richly dressed riders. Behind them were more servants, leading six loaded pack donkeys.

Hezekiah exclaimed, "It's the rich Pharisees doing their Mitzvoth!⁵ Look! Six donkeys! Gee, I've never seen more than three before. They must be carrying lots of goodies!"

When the men got closer John recognized the three mounted on horses. He said, "I've seen those guys before! Those three rich guys came to see John the Baptist. He chewed them out for feasting with King Herod Antipas, even though Herod was in an unlawful marriage with Herodias. He called them a brood of vipers!"

People were running in from the streets in the neighborhood, and gathering at the foot of the synagogue steps. The three men mounted the steps to more fanfare from trumpets, each one preceded by his family flag, and an announcer who proclaimed and extolled his "munificent benefactor." Then each of the three delivered a lengthy speech about the requirements of the law to "do charity," and charged all his listeners to follow his righteous example.

In the meantime, word of the event was spreading through the City of David, and a big crowd was gathering. Servants wearing prominent swords kept order as three lines formed to receive the "goodies." Hezekiah was at the front of one of the lines and picked out food for his family. But alas, there was no new tunic for him among the clothing offered.

Six donkeys could not hold nearly enough for everyone to receive a gift. When the donkey packs were empty, three servants gave out one Hebrew shekel coin to each person who was still in line, while the sword bearers tried to make sure no one got in line twice.

Jesus and the rabbi watched all this from inside the door of the synagogue. When the crowd began to disperse, Jesus called his disciples and Hezekiah to himself, and asked them all a question: "Tell me, will these three men be rewarded for this good work when God's kingdom comes?"

"Yes," said Hezekiah.

"No," said John.

Peter and James were unsure.

Jesus said, "Listen well, then. Be careful not to practice your acts of charity in front of others so you may be seen by them. If you do, you will have no reward from your Father in heaven.

"So when you give to the needy, don't be announcing it with parades and flags and trumpets, as these hypocrites do on the streets and in the synagogues. They want to be honored by other men. Truly I tell you, they have already received their wages, paid in full.

"But when you give to the needy, don't let your left hand know what your right hand is doing, so your giving may be done in secret. Then your Father, who sees what you have done in secret, will reward you." [6]

That evening Jesus, Peter, and the sons of Zebedee arrived back in Gibeah, at the upper room where they had dined on barbecued goat. They were greeted by Peter's wife Concordia and Jesus' mother Mary, who had just arrived from Galilee along with disciple Nathanael and his cousin Matthias. More of Jesus' disciples were also arriving as they gathered for the Feast of Passover.

Mary called out, "Hello, you four! Are you well? We just got in from Ephraim, where we stayed two nights with the Alpheus family. They'll be here in two days with their mother Mary."

She hugged Jesus and John, while Concordia hugged Peter. Concordia said, "My mother Perpetua and our servant

Mina are coming as well. They'll get here with the Alpheus group."

"Wow," said John. "This is gonna be a great Passover! Hezzy and his family are invited too! We're gonna be packed tight in here. This'll be fun!"

3

BETHESDA POOLS

SATURDAY 24 APRIL AD 28, 11:00 AM

Passover was near, and John was walking behind Jesus as they entered Jerusalem unnoticed. They were on their way to the Sheep Gate, which led into the temple courtyards. But first, they were visiting the pair of pools called Bethesda, surrounded by five covered colonnades. Here a great number of Jewish people who weren't permitted in the temple were lying around—those who were blind, lame, crippled, withered, or otherwise disabled.

Many of them were hoping to be cured by the waters of Bethesda. It was said that the water would sometimes stir, and the first person to enter the water while it was stirring would be healed. Jesus talked quietly with some of them, and learned of a man there who was an invalid and had been coming to the pools for the last thirty-eight years.

He found the man lying by one of the pools, and asked him, "Do you want to be made whole?"

"Sir," the man said, "I have no one to help me into the pool when the water stirs. While I am trying to get in, someone else goes down ahead of me."

Then Jesus said to him, "Get up! Pick up your mat and walk." At once the man was made whole. He picked up his mat and began to walk away. A commotion immediately arose among the others who were lying there, and a crowd of passersby began to gather to ask him what happened.

But Jesus and John slipped quietly away into the crowd. [7]

Jesus and John were in the public treasury hall of the temple, between the sanctuary and the Women's Court. Here both men and women could enter to pay the temple tax or give a free will offering. They were sitting on the floor in a corner, and Jesus was watching the people come and go and drop their offerings in the locked moneybox.

Here no lame or blind could enter, for they were barred from the temple. John wondered about that. He said, "Teacher, how do the lame and blind people pay the temple tax?"

Jesus said, "Well, since they're prevented from entering the temple, then they are exempt from the tax. But tell me, little one, why is it the lame and the blind cannot enter the temple? Is there a command in the law of Moses, or in the Prophets, or in the Psalms of David?"

John thought a minute, and in a hesitant voice said, "I… I do remember something from the prophet Samuel about David's House."

"Ah yes, very good, little one. When David was coming into his kingship over all Israel, the Jebusites still held the Citadel of Zion. It was protected by high walls around the mountaintop. The Jebusites mocked David, saying the lame and the blind could protect them, for even a child could throw rocks down on the Israelites from the city walls. King David grew to hate that saying. He told his men to capture the city by climbing up its water tunnel, and to destroy the city's defenders even if they were blind or lame."

"Oh, yes, I remember now, Teacher," said John. "That was when David captured Zion and started calling it the City of David. But didn't they say the lame and blind couldn't come in to David's house?"

"Yes, little one, the prophet tells us that people were saying this. But that was never a command of King David. David didn't hate the lame and the blind. He even invited a man named Mephibosheth, a grandson of King Saul, into his house to live with him and eat with him. And Mephibosheth was crippled in both feet." [8]

John said, "I always thought those people at the Bethesda pools were getting a bad deal. They should be able to come into the temple to pray, just like everyone else."

Jesus said, "The Pharisees, and even some teachers of the Law, hold to many things such as these. They call them the 'tradition of the elders.' I tell you the truth; they set aside the commandments of God so they may follow the traditions of men." [9]

"I think that needs to be fixed," said John.

"I tell you the truth, the time is coming, and in fact is near, when King David's son will enter Jerusalem with a great throng of the lame and blind, and will overturn that false tradition," said Jesus. "On that day many will be healed in the temple who were never healed at Bethesda."

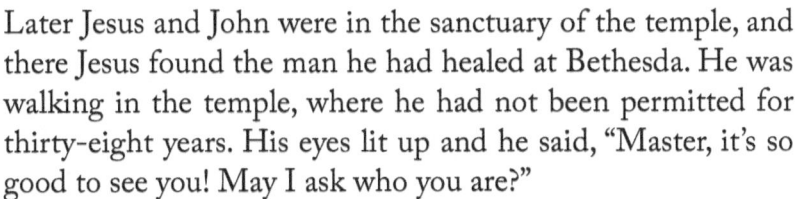

Later Jesus and John were in the sanctuary of the temple, and there Jesus found the man he had healed at Bethesda. He was walking in the temple, where he had not been permitted for thirty-eight years. His eyes lit up and he said, "Master, it's so good to see you! May I ask who you are?"

"I am Jesus of Nazareth," he said.

"I am Elias of Bethany. The temple officials have been scolding me. They told me I was forbidden to carry my mat, because it's the Sabbath," he said. "But I told them that the man who healed me said to pick up my mat and walk. They asked me who that was, but I didn't know. They were angry over your instructions to me."

Jesus said, "Do not be disturbed by them. See, you are well again. Now repent and free your life from sin, or something worse may happen to you." [10]

Jesus and John made their way to Solomon's Colonnade on the east side of the temple courts, overlooking the Mount of Olives. There Jesus sat down and began to teach with words from Scripture. At first John was his only pupil, but slowly a group began to grow around Jesus. The people said, "We've never heard anything like this! He teaches as a man of authority!"

Some of them recognized this was Jesus of Nazareth, and the word of his presence in the temple began to spread. By the time Jesus left at sundown, some two hundred men and women had gathered round to hear Jesus teach.

4

Adultery Forgiven

SUNDAY 25 APRIL AD 28, 6:00 AM

The sun was just beginning to rise when Jesus entered the temple courts again, followed only by John. He went again to Solomon's Colonnade, overlooking the Mount of Olives. People were arriving to attend the morning sacrifice, and a group of Levites was leaving the temple sanctuary after keeping watch in the all-night vigil.[11] Many people gathered around Jesus, as he sat down and began teaching.

When the temple service was over, a group of men—Pharisees and teachers of the Law—came over and approached Jesus. They were escorting a woman wearing a hooded cloak, who was looking down at the ground. Jesus rose to meet them.

One of them greeted Jesus, and said, "Teacher, this woman has been caught in adultery, in the very act. In the Law, Moses commanded us to stone such women to death.[12] Now what do you say?"

John wondered at this. He thought, *"Why are they bringing this woman to Jesus? Are they trying to trap him in his words?"*

But Jesus said nothing. He bent down and began writing in the dust on the ground with his finger. They watched him in silence for a time, and then pressed their question again: "Do you not uphold the Law? Should this woman be stoned, or not?"

Jesus straightened up and said to them, "If any one among you is without sin, let him be the first to throw a stone at her." And Jesus again bent down, writing on the ground.

At this, the crowd moved away from the woman so they would not be injured by any misguided stones. There was a prolonged silence, hanging heavy in the air. As the silence continued, all those who had heard Jesus began to go away, one at a time—the oldest ones first. Finally, only Jesus was left, with the woman still standing there.

Jesus straightened up and asked her, "Woman, where are they? Has no one condemned you?"

"No one, Lord," she said.

"Then neither do I condemn you," Jesus declared. "Go now, and leave your life of sin behind." [13]

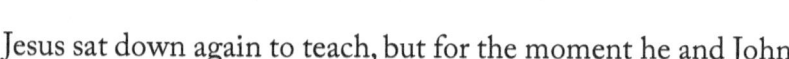

Jesus sat down again to teach, but for the moment he and John were alone.

"Teacher," John asked, "what was that you were writing in the dust?"

"Little one, I was praying to my Father in heaven to reveal to each person here their own sin."

"Oh," John said. Then he knew why he had felt so unworthy during the long silence.

Later the rest of the disciples from Gibeah joined them, and a crowd again gathered around Jesus as he taught about the coming kingdom of God.

5

SON OF GOD

MONDAY 26 APRIL AD 28, 4:30 AM

In the early morning darkness Jesus entered the torch-lit temple courts, followed by John and twenty-three more disciples. Today was the day before Passover, so the courts were already busy with visitors from all across the Roman Empire: Jewish men and women from Rome, Greece, Asia Minor, Syria, and especially Egypt.

Jesus led his men into the temple to participate in the prayers at the morning sacrifice, while Concordia used the separate entrance into the women's court. A chorus of Levites was singing psalms as they ended the overnight vigil, and the disciples joined in the song. Then the priests assigned to the morning watch arrived and began the service.

After the service, Jesus and the disciples threaded through the crowd to Solomon's Colonnade, where Jesus sat down to teach. Some of the Pharisees had noticed Jesus in the temple and followed behind the disciples. Among them, John saw the two Pharisees who had challenged Jesus in Gibeah about his disciples "preparing food" on the Sabbath.

An elder Pharisee approached Jesus and said, "Teacher, we have heard of things you and your disciples have been doing on the Sabbath that appear to violate Moses' law. We have also heard that you supported these actions when you were questioned about them. How do you defend yourself from these accusations?"

Jesus said, "My Father is always at his work to this very day, and I too am working."

Another Pharisee said, "But your father Joseph is not with us."

A third one said, "Do you mean to make yourself equal to the One God by calling yourself his Son? That is an outrageous claim, and may earn you a death sentence for blasphemy!"

Jesus paused, and then said: "Truly I tell you, the Son can do nothing by himself; he can do only what he sees his Father doing. What the Father does, the Son does. The Father loves the Son and shows him everything he does, and will show him even greater things that will astound you. The Father raises the dead and gives them life, so also the Son gives life to those he chooses. Not only that, but the Father has given all judgment to the Son, so the Son may be honored just as the Father. Whoever fails to honor the Son fails to honor the Father who sent him. If any of you have ears to hear, let him hear."

The eldest Pharisee gasped, and a look of dismay came over his face. When he had composed himself, he said, "Jesus of Nazareth, I warn you, the path you are choosing will lead to your condemnation. We cannot honor a mere man in the same way we honor God. I will not now call the temple police and disturb this great crowd of pilgrims who have come for Passover. But I do charge you; think well on what you are saying." And he turned and left Jesus, followed by the whole group of Pharisees.

The crowd that had gathered pressed closer to Jesus, to hear how he might respond. Peter and James positioned themselves on both sides of Jesus. The moment was tense.

Jesus addressed the crowd: "You have heard these men. They study the Scriptures diligently because they think that in them they have eternal life. Yet those are the very Scriptures that testify about me, and they still refuse to come to me to have life. Truly I say to you all; everyone who hears my words and believes I am from the Father has eternal life. They will not face judgment, for they have crossed over from death into life."

This caused a stir in the crowd, and a hush fell over the courtyard to see what he might say next. Jesus paused for a long moment of silence, and then continued earnestly: "Truly I tell you, the time has come when the dead will hear the voice of the Son of God and those who hear will live. Do not be amazed at this, for the time is coming when all those who are in their graves will hear his voice and come out. Those who have done what is good will rise to live, and those who have done what is evil will rise to be condemned."[14]

———•••●••———

Nathanael, Andrew, and John were ahead of the rest, arriving back in Gibeah before sunset. John exclaimed, "Hey, look, there's Tad and his dad!"

James son of Alpheus, his brother Joses, and son Thaddeus were coming down the outside stairs of the upper room. Tad said, "Hey, John! Good to see you guys! We're on our way to the temple to sing at the vigil before Passover."

John said, "Wow, you're a son of the Law, now, aren't you? You'll be serving at the temple as a full-up Levite, not a kid anymore! We just came from the temple; Jesus has been teaching there all day."

Little James said, "Well, if Jesus spent the whole day teaching at the temple, I'm sure there's going to be a lot of gossip to catch up on. Some of the Levites are well connected to what's going on in the inner circle of temple chiefs."

"We'll be expecting a full report," said Nathanael wryly. "You're right about the gossip, though. Go with God. You'll be passing most of the disciples coming this way."

The Alpheus trio started up the road to Jerusalem while the three young Galileans climbed the stairs. Inside, they found the rest of the Alpheus family: Matthew and his wife Paula and their six children, including Matthew Junior and Sarah and their grandmother Mary. Perpetua and Mina were also there, all hosted by Mary the mother of Jesus.

They had barely sat down when Peter, Big James, and Concordia came in the door. Concordia exclaimed, "Mother! How was your trip?"

Perpetua said, "Not bad at all. But we're hungry. Is anyone preparing food?"

Jesus' mother Mary said, "Our hosts downstairs are getting the food ready. There will be thirty-five of us to feed tonight."

Mary Alpheus said, "Well, let's go down and see what we can do to help! Sarah, watch after the kids; don't let them get into any trouble." And the six women disappeared down the stairs.

John greeted Matthew Junior: "Hey Matt! You should hear what's been happening this week! Andrew and I got chased out of a farmer's field, then the farmer got a couple of Pharisees to complain to Jesus about us!" The two of them sat down in a corner of the room, joined by Andrew and Nathanael, and John told Matt the story of the farmer's field and the Pharisees.

"Not only that," John continued, "but those two Pharisees brought in reinforcements today when Jesus was teaching in the temple. They brought one of the elders of the Pharisees to give Jesus a lecture about healing people on the Sabbath."

Judas of Kerioth arrived in the room and heard John talking about Jesus, so he came over to listen to the conversation.

Matt asked John, "So what did Jesus say to the elder Pharisee?"

"He said he's just doing the same thing his Father is doing. But you've heard Jesus: when he talks about his Father, he means his Father in heaven. They told him he's making himself out to be equal to God."

Matt said, "That sounds like a dangerous thing for him to say in the temple."

"Yea," John agreed, "the elder Pharisee threatened him with the death penalty. Nate, what do you think? Can they kill him for what he said?"

Nathanael said, "Not very likely. They were mostly bluffing. First of all, they couldn't arrest him in the middle of that big crowd; it would've started a riot. Somebody would've been hurt, and the people would've blamed the Pharisees for it."

Andrew asked, "So does that mean they can arrest him if they find him alone?"

Nathanael said, "Well yes, but that doesn't mean they would succeed if they brought him to trial before the Supreme Council. I listened very closely to what Jesus was saying. He never actually said the words, 'I am the Son of God.'

"If they brought him to trial, the witnesses probably wouldn't be able to agree on what Jesus actually said. And even if they got the words right, there would be Pharisees and others who wouldn't agree it was enough to convict him of blasphemy. The evidence rules are very strict for a death penalty case.

"And besides all that, Roman law doesn't let Jews perform the death penalty anyway. The trial would fail, and people would make fun of the Pharisees for losing."

John smiled. "Maybe that's the worst thing that can happen to a Pharisee," he said, "for people to make fun of them. They always want to be taken so seriously."

Nathanael smiled also. "But they've already started this argument, and they're not going to give up easily. In their eyes, Jesus is trying to destroy the Sabbath and make himself equal to God by calling God his own Father. They're going to keep trying to trap him in his words, or find some other way to get him killed. An unlucky accident on a lonely street would suit them just fine, but there's no way they would want to be blamed for that."

Judas of Kerioth joined in. He said, "They can't kill Jesus. I've seen the power of this man. I believe he could say a single word and it would flatten a whole platoon of Roman soldiers. He's just waiting for the right time: like he says, 'when the time is fulfilled.'"

6

ANOTHER PASSOVER

WEDNESDAY 28 APRIL AD 28, 11:00 AM

"Simon, where is everybody?" Nathanael asked. "Not all the disciples are here. You're in charge of the head count, aren't you?" Andrew and the sons of Zebedee were also relaxing outside with Nathanael, while the smell of roast lamb was beginning to hover over the town of Gibeah.

Simon, the former Zealot, said, "Yes, Nate, that's my assignment. My job was to spread the news to all the disciples and have them meet here for Passover. I sent Joseph *bar* Sabbas to round up the last twelve of them from Judea, and they're on their way. Joseph went down the coast through Jamnia and Ashkelon, and he's coming back up through Beersheba and Hebron. They're supposed to get here by noon today."

James and Joses the sons of Alpheus came down the stairs, followed by Thaddeus, who was blinking and yawning. "Wow, Tad, you look sleepy," said John. "How was the vigil?"

"It was great," Tad said. "We sang most all the psalms of David. But I'm not used to staying up all night."

Nathanael said, "Did you guys hear any scuttlebutt about Jesus and the Pharisees?"

Little James said, "We sure did. For one thing, there was a man at Bethesda healed by Jesus on the Sabbath. He told the temple officials it was Jesus who healed him, and the Pharisees added that to their complaints about him."

"I have a feeling their complaint list is going to keep on growing," said Nathanael.

"Yes, but something more dangerous is going on. The Pharisees are talking about asking the party of the Herodians to help destroy Jesus. They're impressed with the success they had in getting John the Baptist thrown in prison, when the Sadducees asked for their help. That stopped him from preaching, and the Sadducees didn't even get blamed for it. The people who believe John is a prophet are blaming Governor Pilate for handing him over to Herod." [15]

Big James said, "We need to keep an eye out for troublemakers when we're with Jesus. Peter and I have been sticking close by his side when he's traveling."

"Speaking of Jesus," said Nathanael, "where is he? I haven't seen him around today."

John said, "I saw him this morning when he left to go up into the hills to walk and pray. I think he'll be back pretty soon."

Simon interrupted, "Hey, here comes Joseph and his group now!"

The Judeans arrived with Joseph *bar* Sabbas, rounding out the number of disciples to forty in all: thirty-nine men and one woman. They exchanged greetings with the group around Nathanael, and with other disciples coming down the stairs.

Joseph said, "I don't know how you guys stand it. The smell of roast lamb is everywhere. It's still a long time till supper, and I'm hungry!"

John spotted a family coming down the road. He shouted out, "Hezzy! Welcome! Glad you're here!" John and Andrew greeted Abigail and her children, including Deborah, now eighteen months old.

Then Matthew the former tax collector came down with his sons, and with Peter, Philip, Thomas, and Judas. That left only women upstairs, including Concordia, Matthew's daughter Sarah, and the others.

Matthew spoke to Hezekiah's mother: "Are you Abigail? The other women want you to come up and join them. I don't know what they're up to. They kicked all the men out."

Abigail went up the stairs with baby Deborah and her two little girls. John introduced Hezzy, David, and Dan—ages ten, eight, and seven, to Mathew's younger sons Amram, Izhar, Hebron, and Uzziel—ages eleven, nine, seven, and five. The children immediately began to run around and play with a willow hoop that Matthew Junior made for them.

And Jesus was sitting under a fig tree watching them. John had no idea how Jesus could have gotten there without anyone noticing him. John went over and sat down beside him. "Teacher, I didn't see you here," said John.

Jesus chuckled. "I know. I've been listening to all of you talk for a while now."

John was embarrassed. "I hope I didn't say anything wrong," he said.

Jesus chuckled again. "You should hope that all the time, little one, for the Father hears every word you say. Oh, look, Abigail is coming down the stairs."

Indeed she was, followed by the other women. She was wearing bright, colorful new clothing, and her face was shining like the sun. The difference from her old stained clothing was stunning. Following behind, her girls were also wearing new clothes, even toddler Deborah, who was being carried down the stairs by Jesus' mother Mary.

Abigail called out, "Gather 'round, my boys. Grandma Alpheus has something for each of you."

Helped by Concordia, Mary the mother of James and Joses gave new clothing to Dan and David. The two boys jumped up and down, shouting with joy and thankfulness. "Now go on upstairs, boys, and get dressed," said Concordia.

Hezekiah looked uncomfortable and confused. Mary Alpheus took a new tunic from Concordia, and said, "Hezekiah son of Malchiel, this tunic was made especially for you, by a girl in Joppa who heard of your hospitality toward Jesus. It has no seams, for she wove it as a single piece of cloth. It's salt-and-pepper colored, made from the wool of white and black sheep, so it will be easy to care for. Wear it proudly."

Hezekiah was stunned. He took the tunic and held it out to look at it. It was just his size. He was speechless, with tears rolling down his face. He couldn't say a word.

"Now, where's Jesus?" said his mother Mary. "Oh, there you are! Son, there is something here for you also."

Jesus got up and walked over to mother Alpheus who presented him with a new tunic. It was also made of a single woven piece of cloth, and it was brilliant white, as white as could be bleached by the best laundry-person in the land. Mary said, "This was woven by a girl in Joppa who has never seen you, yet she tells everyone she meets that you are the Son of God."

Jesus looked deeply touched. John noticed he was wearing the same faded tunic as the first time John saw him. Jesus said, "Many have seen, but most blessed is she who has not seen, and those who will never see, yet still will believe."

Jesus and Hezekiah went up to change. And John was about to celebrate his fifteenth Passover.

7

THE WITHERED HAND

SATURDAY 1 MAY AD 28, 8:00 AM

"Judas, the Passover Feast was wonderful," said John. They were on their way to the morning synagogue service in Gibeah. It was going to be filled to the doorsteps, owing to the attendance of the disciples and their family members.

"Yes, John, we ate well," said Judas. "But I had to pay for the provisions out of our moneybag, and it's empty now. Our hosts have fed us since Passover, but they're beginning to tire of us. Tomorrow we'll be on the road to Galilee, and I have no idea what we're going to eat. And I'm ashamed to bring this problem to Jesus."

John said, "But if we take the high road, the folks in Ephraim and Sychar will feed us."

Judas said, "You may be right. But if we go back the way we came, on the low road through Jericho, I'm going to be picking the disciple's pockets."

Jesus went into the synagogue and was teaching during the service. A man was there whose right hand was shriveled, and a group of Pharisees from Jerusalem were watching to see what Jesus would do. After the service, they gathered around

Jesus and one of them asked, "Teacher, is it lawful to heal on the Sabbath?"

John thought, "*This sounds like another trap.*"

Jesus said, "I ask you, which is lawful on the Sabbath: to do good or to do evil? Is it lawful to save life, or destroy it?" But they remained silent. Jesus looked around at them angrily.

So Jesus said, "If one of you has a sheep and it falls into a pit on the Sabbath, won't you take hold of it and lift it out? How much more valuable then is a person than a sheep! So you see, it is lawful to do good on the Sabbath."

Then Jesus turned and said to the man with the shriveled hand, "Get up and stand in front of everyone." So he got up and stood there.

Then Jesus said, "Now stretch out your hand." So he stretched it out and his hand was completely restored, just as sound as the other. But the Pharisees and teachers of the Law were angry and left the synagogue discussing what they might do.[16]

That evening, "Little" James son of Alpheus came up the stairs looking for Peter, and found him sitting next to John and "Big" James son of Zebedee. "Peter, there's trouble brewing," he said worriedly. "There's a chance that a squad of temple police may come to Gibeah tomorrow to try to arrest Jesus."

Peter responded, "Oh, no, I was afraid of that. But I didn't think they would come out here."

"Neither did I. Technically, they don't have authority out here," said Little James.

Peter said, "Well they can look, but they won't find us. Jesus is putting us on the road before dawn."

8

Escape

SUNDAY 2 MAY AD 28, 4:00 AM

Big James shook his brother by the shoulder. "Wake up, little brother, it's time to pack up for the road," he said.

"Mmmphff," John mumbled. "Where's Jesus?"

"I just passed him when I was coming up the stairs. He went out to pray."

"Oh, rats. I wanted to go with him. You were on night watch?"

"Yes. Peter and I and Judas and the Zealot each took a watch. But I felt a little pathetic carrying only a shepherd's club, and watching for a squad of cops carrying swords."

John said, "I think maybe Jesus is watching over us, not us watching over him."

"You're right John, but I still feel better when we have someone on guard."

Within an hour the forty disciples packed up for the road, and Matt Junior would be going with them. Jesus had indicated they would be walking the low road along the Jordan River.[17]

Thomas and Matthew Senior were staying behind for a couple hours to help Paula, Perpetua, Mina, and Jesus' mother load up two donkeys for their journey on the upper road. Matthew's younger children were invited by their grandmother to visit at Ephraim, and the women were going with them. They would be travelling with a group of men returning to Galilee from the Passover Feast in Jerusalem.

Jesus was back from his walk, and led the disciples out of the building. When he reached the bottom of the stairs, three women of Gibeah came up to him and laid three small moneybags at his feet. Judas picked them up and carried them.

They were almost to Jericho when Matthew Senior and Thomas caught up to the group. John said, "Hi, Mathew. Did you get your family off safely from Gibeah?"

"Yes we did," he said. "But you should hear what Thomas did."

"Oh yeah? Tell me, Thomas."

Thomas said, "Just like Little James thought, ten temple police wearing big swords came looking for Jesus. I told them I just saw a big group of Galileans going north on the upper road, which was true. They took off down that road looking for Jesus."

"They'll be wasting their time today," said Matthew. "From Gibeon it's over ten miles to Samaria, and that's where they'll have to turn around. When they get back to Jerusalem they're going to be late for dinner, and they'll be empty-handed."

9

ROADIES

THURSDAY 6 MAY AD 28, 4:00 PM

John, Andrew, Philip, Nate, Tad, and Matt—the six teenagers among the disciples—were resting on the sandy beach at Bethabara beside the Jordan River. They were at the place where John the Baptist had been preaching last year, and were camping in the shade of the low trees and bushes. Jesus had been leading them on a leisurely pace along the river, spending time with his disciples. When they passed by Jericho, Judas and the Zealot had gone into the city to buy fresh bread for the disciples.

John said, "We've still got plenty of food left, with this bread Judas bought. Most of the guys already had their packs stuffed with leftovers from Gibeah."

"Yeah, no complaints," said Andrew. "Hey, Nate, who are those six guys you and Philip were talking to on the road? They've been following us since Jericho."

Nathanael said, "They're Greek-speaking pilgrims from Tyre and Sidon returning from the Passover Feast. In Jerusalem they heard about 'Jesus of Nazareth' and want to know what he's all about. My guess is they'll keep following us until they hear Jesus preach."

Philip said, "They don't speak Aramaic very well. I might have to translate Jesus' teaching into Greek for them."

Matt spoke up. "I've heard you speaking Greek, Philip. You sound like you came straight from the land of Greece. How'd you learn that?"

Philip said, "My mom is a Greek. She came straight from Greece before she married my dad, and she taught me how to read and write and pronounce the language like a Greek."

John said, "Those aren't the only ones following us. There must be thirty people hanging with us."

"Yeah," said Nate. "When travelers from Jerusalem catch up with us they don't pass us by. They're mostly from Galilee and Trachonitis, but a few are from Judea, or east of the Jordan, or even from way south in Idumea. They must have come looking for Jesus."

Andrew said, "I think it's all about the healing of that man with the withered hand, right in the Pharisees' faces. Jesus was defiant when he was making that point."

Nate said, "You may be right. But I met a couple guys who came because they heard about the police trying to arrest him. I told them the Pharisees didn't have enough evidence to kill him, so they want to throw him in prison to shut him up."

"That's comical," said Matt. "They wanted to silence Jesus and all they did was make him famous."

John said, "That's not the only thing. A few sick people have come up to Jesus, and he healed them. They tell the others, and then travelers who were just trying to get home decide to hang with Jesus for a while instead."[18]

When the group left Bethabara, the number of disciples had increased from forty to forty-one, for Jesus had called Matt to follow him. John and Andrew baptized Matt in the same pool where they had been immersed by John the Baptist.

10

GROUPIES

SUNDAY 9 MAY AD 28, 7:00 AM

John and Jesus were returning to the disciples' campsite on the south shore of the Sea of Galilee after an early morning walk. Today would be their final push toward Capernaum, on the northeast shore of the lake. The disciples had enjoyed a full week of fellowship with Jesus, but now the food in their packs was running low. John had a question.

"Teacher, are we all going to stay in Capernaum? We might not all fit in Peter's house."

"Yes, little one, but you're forgetting Matthew's house. His upper room could fit all of us if it were needed. And speaking of Peter, find him and tell him it's time to get everyone on the road."

"Yes sir," said John. "Are we going to stop at the hot springs?"

"We will see what the Father has in store for us there."

The Hammath hot springs, known for their curative properties, were two miles north of where they were camped, and the city wall of Tiberias was only a mile past that. John had been to the springs several times with his father Zebedee, who said the hot water stopped his old bones from aching. Several visitors from both the springs and the city had already come to see the disciples, and word was beginning to spread that Jesus was back in Galilee.

Jesus was at the front with Peter and James on the road that passes the springs, and John was walking behind them with his friends. But the road ahead was blocked. Standing, sitting, and lying in the roadway were a dozen people, both men and women, many of them elderly. When they saw Jesus they called out, "Master, help us!"

Jesus said, "What do you want me to do for you?"

A middle-aged woman said, "Great teacher, we want to be healed of our infirmities."

"Woman, tell me your name," said Jesus.

"I am Susanna of Sennabris, a town not far from here. I suffer from curling down of my toes. It began when I was a child, and every year it gets worse. It is painful for me to walk."

"Do you believe I can heal you?"

"Yes, Master, I do."

Jesus stretched out his hand to touch her outstretched hand. "Let it be as you said. Be strong and walk, and give thanks to God for your release from weakness." Immediately her toes were relaxed and straightened, and she had no pain. One at a time, Jesus touched each of the others, and healed them all. They began praising God in thankfulness for their recovery.

They left the hot springs with the rest of the disciples, followed by the crowd that had gathered during their short vacation along the Jordan River. Susanna and others who had been healed at the springs joined them. They were bypassing

Tiberias, following the road that skirted the city's western wall. But ahead of them, the roadway was blocked again!

A group of twenty or more Jews from the city were waiting outside the main gate for them, spilling across the road. Tiberias had been built over a graveyard, and was considered unclean for Jews. But some had begun to live there anyway. They were mostly servants and government employees of King Herod Antipas.

Two of them called out, "Jesus, Master, heal our sickness, please!" Jesus paused to learn of their need, and placed his hands on them to make them well. While he was healing, John noticed a finely dressed but hooded woman hanging at the back of the group, looking uneasy and apprehensive.

Jesus called out to her. "Joanna, daughter of Abraham, wife of Chuza, step forward." A murmur rose among the surrounding people. Chuza the Syrian was Herod Antipas' property manager in charge of his personal land holdings, and was widely despised.

Joanna stepped forward timidly, with an eleven-year-old boy close behind her.

Now that she was closer, John could see that beneath her hood she had bruises on her face, and a black eye. Jesus spoke tenderly to her, "Joanna, do you not wish for healing?"

"Yes, my Lord," she replied softly. "But my husband will just hit me again, for no reason."

Jesus was visibly moved. He laid his hands on her head and said, "Woman, your Father in heaven has greater things for you than this. Be healed of your injuries, and follow me."

Immediately John could see her face was clear and shining, unbruised.

Jesus turned to his disciples saying, "Concordia, walk with Joanna for a while, and watch over her." He laid his hand on the shoulder of Joanna's son, and said, "John, walk with young Michael here, and spend some time with him."

Concordia came forward and embraced Joanna, who collapsed sobbing into Concordia's arms.

"I'm sorry," Joanna said, "I'm just so afraid."

Jesus led them around Tiberias and east to the shore of the Sea of Galilee, where he paused for a bit. Concordia and Joanna were talking softly, and John was introducing his friends to Michael, who was concerned for his mother.

The bustling commercial city of Magdala was ahead, and Jesus was leading them on the road that would pass through the middle of town. On the left side of the road were modest but comfortable houses, many of them with an upper deck or upper room overlooking the lake. On the right side were boat slips and fishing gear shops with technicians who were manufacturing or repairing fishing equipment and nets. There were also worksites with master craftsmen who were building new boats for sale, from small rowboats to sailing ships as long as thirty feet.

Jobs were plentiful here, especially at the fish packing plant, a smelly and low-paying job. From Magdala dried and salted fish were packed into large clay jars, and shipped overseas as far away as Rome. John recalled father Zebedee's joke: "If a fish-packer is coming to dine at your house, you will have plenty of time to prepare the food, for the aroma will arrive long before the guest."

When they entered the city, they saw the road lined with people on both sides, as if they were spectators for a parade. By the time they reached the harbor, the spectators were falling in behind them and becoming part of the parade. They were approaching the fish packing plant, and it seemed its entire staff had emptied out of the building to see Jesus pass by. A great many of the fish packers were women, who had little chance of other employment if they had no husband.

The women were expectant and excited, but one of them appeared disturbed and agitated. Abruptly she ran up to Jesus and called out loudly—in a strange other-worldly voice—"What do you want with us, Jesus of Nazareth? We know who you are—the Son of the almighty God!"

Immediately Jesus demanded, "Be quiet! Tell me your name!"

The reply came back, "Our name is Shebuah, for we are sevened."

"Shebuah, depart from this woman, all seven of you, and be cast into the sea never to return!"

At once the woman became completely limp, and collapsed in a heap onto the street.

Concordia, Joanna, and Susanna were near Jesus, and came to attend to the stricken woman. They helped her to her feet, for she was dazed and speechless. "Follow me," said Jesus.[19]

As they passed the Magdala synagogue, people on its steps were expecting Jesus to enter and teach, but Jesus continued past. Some two hundred people were following him now, but the synagogue building was only twenty-five feet square.

As Jesus advanced onto the Plain of Kinnereth, many from the city of Magdala followed him, and another crowd was approaching from Capernaum to the north. Boats from Magdala were following offshore, and more boats were coming from Capernaum. John didn't see his father Zebedee's boat among them, but he did spot his coworkers Beon and Bohan in their rowboat. These two sons of Bashan were fishermen like himself.

Jesus went down with the crowds and stood on a level place next to the shore. Because of the crowd he told his disciples to have a boat standing ready for him, to keep the people from crowding him. Peter and James signaled to Beon and Bohan to row in close to shore.

People from Tyre and Sidon, Idumea, Galilee, and beyond Jordan—from north, south, east and west—had come to hear Jesus and to be healed of their diseases. The more people he healed, the more would push forward to try to touch him, for power was flowing from him and healing them all. When those troubled by foul spirits saw him, they fell down before him and cried out, "You are the Son of God." But he gave them strict orders to keep silent.[20]

Jesus healed and taught until nightfall. Then he sent the disciples and the three new women followers to Matthew's house for an evening meal, while he went up to the mountainside to spend the night praying alone.

11

JESUS AND THE TWELVE

MONDAY 10 MAY AD 28, 5:00 AM

John slipped away early, taking care no one from yesterday's crowds saw him. He was climbing the upper terrain behind Capernaum, looking for Jesus in the high places where he would often pray. The last couple days had been a rush of activity, and Jesus himself hadn't had a chance to eat since yesterday morning.

"John! Over here!" It was Jesus, calling John to him from a nearby hillock.

John said, "Teacher! I'm glad to find you!" John went over to where Jesus was sitting.

Jesus said, "It's good you came. I want you to tell certain disciples to come up to me now. The rest may come up after they've had a bite to eat." And he related a list of twelve names.

"Yes, sir," said John, and he hurried back to town. Some of the disciples on the list were at Matthew's house, but most were at Peter's. They set out together climbing into the hills.

Jesus smiled broadly as the twelve arrived. "Ah, you have come to me," he said. "Did you know no one is able come to me except it be given by the Father? You and my other followers are a cherished gift.

"But from my followers I have chosen you twelve. I have elected you to be with me and to go with me during my travels. I will have other followers, but you will be close by my side.

"You are the twelve precious stones of the people of God, the pillars of the assembly that will bear my name. Today I appoint you as emissaries—my representatives—to be sent on missions in my name, to preach both near and far, both now and later.

"Listen now to the blessings that will befall you in the days to come:

"Simon son of Jonah, you will be revered always as Peter, the rock—shepherd of my flock.

"Andrew son of Jonah, you will preach Good News to Scythia, and oversee Byzantium.

"James son of Zebedee, you will be the first of the twelve to glorify my name.

"John son of Zebedee, you will be the last of the twelve to glorify my name.

"Philip of Bethsaida, you will preach good news to Greeks wherever you find them.

"Nathanael son of Tolmai, fearless to speak the truth, you will preach to kings in Armenia.

"Judas Thomas, called the Twin, you will add sheep to my flock in India.

"Matthew son of Alpheus, instead of collecting taxes for Caesar you will collect disciples for the *Son of Man*, and your testimony about me will be taught in all the corners of the earth.

"James son of Alpheus, you will preach good news in Egypt and in Persia.

"Judas Thaddeus son of James, you will preach in Syria. Those with lost causes will turn to you.

"Simon my Zealot, your zeal will take you to preach good news in Africa and England.

"Judas, son of Simon man of Kerioth, by your hand the will of the Father concerning me will be accomplished, but when it takes place it will pierce your heart."[21]

12

Rock Star

TUESDAY 11 MAY AD 28, 8:00 AM

The next day, Jesus was headed down the hillside, followed by all his disciples. He had spoken to them on the hill, and had welcomed the three newly healed women into his band of disciples.

But as they descended, from the base of the hills hundreds of people were approaching. There were even more people than had crowded around him at the lakeshore last night. The way back to Capernaum was effectively blocked. Jesus looked around. Seeing a hilltop nearby, he climbed it and sat on a large rock. Peter and Big James had the disciples sit down around him in a circle, so the arriving throng would not be crowding the Master. John sat down with Tad, Matt, and Michael, expectantly listening.

When the people had settled in, Jesus looked directly at his disciples and began to teach, saying:

"Blessed are you who are poor, for yours is the kingdom of God.

"Blessed are you who hunger now, for you will be satisfied.

"Blessed are you who mourn and weep now, for you will laugh.

"Blessed are you when you are hated and persecuted, and all kinds of false evil is said against you because of me. For in the same way they persecuted the true prophets who came before you. Rejoice in that day and leap for joy, because great is your reward in heaven.

"But Woe!

"Woe to you who are rich, for you have already received your reward.

"Woe to you who are well fed now, for you will go hungry.

"Woe to you who laugh now, for you will mourn and weep.

"Woe to you when everyone speaks well of you, for that is how your fathers treated the false prophets who led God's people astray.

"You have heard it said, 'Love your neighbor, and hate your enemy.' But to you who have ears to hear, I say: Love your enemies. Do good to those who hate you. Bless those who curse you. Pray for those who mistreat you. In this way you may be children of your Father in heaven, who causes his sun to rise on the evil and the good, and sends rain for the righteous and the unrighteous.

"If you only love those who love you, what credit is that to you? Don't even the tax collectors do that? And if you greet only your own people, what are you doing more than others? Don't even the godless peoples do that?

"If someone slaps you on the cheek, turn to him the other cheek also. If someone takes your coat, don't hold back your shirt from him. Give to everyone who asks of you. If anyone takes what belongs to you, don't demand it back. Treat others the same way you want others to treat you.

"Then your reward will be great, and you will be children of the Most High, because he is kind, even to the ungrateful and the wicked. Be merciful, just as your Father is merciful. Be perfect, just as your Father in heaven is perfect." [22]

Jesus looked around at the crowd surrounding his disciples, and said, "Some of you are my followers, and some of you desire to be my followers. But why would you call me 'Lord, Lord,' and then not do what I say?

"For each one who comes and hears my words and acts on them, I'll show you what he is like:

"He is like the wise man who built his house on a rock. And the rains fell, and the floods came, and the winds blew and howled against that house; but it didn't fall, for it had been founded upon the rock.

"But for each one who hears my words but does not act upon them, he is like the foolish man who built his house on the sand. The rains fell, the floods came, and the winds blew and howled against that house, and it collapsed, and great was the ruin of that house.

"So I say to all you men and women, listen well, and remember these words as you walk your way. Narrow is the path and small is the gate leading to life, and few find it. But broad is the highway and wide is the gate leading to destruction, and many enter through it."

When Jesus had finished all these words, the crowds were amazed, for he was teaching them as one who had authority, not as a student of Scripture like their teachers of the Law. [23]

Jesus had Peter and Big James open up a corridor so people could come forward and be healed, and Jesus healed them all, and cast out any foul spirits they held. Jesus continued healing and talking softly with those who came forward throughout the day. It seemed to John there was an endless number of them.

As the sun began to set, Jesus dismissed the people, and went with his disciples back to Capernaum for an evening meal.

John sat down to eat with Matt, who was eager to talk: "My dad says that this week Jesus fulfilled a prophecy of Isaiah by proclaiming justice for Jews and non-Jews alike, without quarreling or shouting, but by healing them all and giving them hope."

John said, "I might know the scripture he means, where God chooses his beloved servant." [24]

"Yes. And he also found out from Jesus' mother that Jesus was born in Bethlehem. The prophet Micah wrote that the Messiah would come from Bethlehem.[25] My dad is carrying ink and parchment to take notes of what Jesus teaches and does. I think he's going to write a book about Jesus. He gets excited when Jesus does something that fulfills a prophecy from Holy Scripture."

"Oh, that would be great," said John. "I can't wait to read it."

13

MARY OF MAGDALA

WEDNESDAY 12 MAY AD 28, 5:00 PM

John, Nate, and Philip were in the courtyard of Peter's house waiting for dinner to be announced, when Concordia came in from outside, along with Susanna of Sennabris.

"Hi, ladies," said Nathanael, "What have you two been up to?"

Concordia said, "We've been down in Magdala trying to learn something about Mary, and how she became plagued by seven demons. She's still in shock from what happened to her and doesn't want to talk just yet. She seems really fragile right now."

"You're right about that," said Philip. "Did you find out anything?"

"Yes, quite a lot," Concordia said. "She showed up in Magdala two years ago looking really beat up. Wherever she ran away from, it seems someone wanted her killed. They call her 'Mary' but that isn't her real name. The wife of the mayor in Magdala put her under the mayor's protection and arranged her job at the fish packing plant. She can outpack anyone else in the plant, but no one there knows her family, or her clan, or her tribe."

Nathanael said, "Well, she's clearly a Galilean, from her accent. Is that all you learned?"

"No, there's more. We just came from talking with Portia, the wife of Lord Mayor Jaroel here in Capernaum. It turns out that Portia had helped her get some clothing and find a place for her to stay in Magdala.

"Portia found out the girl had been pledged by her parents to marry an older man in her home town, but she rejected the man and refused to marry him. Her parents were furious, and threw her out of the house, saying she was no longer their daughter. Then some friends of the groom got together and did terrible things to her in revenge. When they had finished they told her that, now, she would be worthless to any man for the rest of her life, and no man would want her."

John was shocked. "Oh, that's awful! How could anyone do that?"

Susanna said, "You'd be surprised what some men will do when they think their honor has been insulted. They can be very cruel."

"How is she doing?" said Concordia. "I left her with my mom and Paula."

"She and Joanna have been spending time together and striking up a friendship," said John.

"Oh, that's just what she needs right now," said Concordia.

"I guess we'll find out later how she picked up the company of seven demons," said Philip.

"Yea, I'd like to know more about that," said John.

"It's nothing to worry about right now," said Susanna. "That will come out when she's ready to talk about it. Oh look, here comes Mina—dinner must be ready."

14

The Centurion's Servant

SUNDAY 29 MAY AD 28, 10:00 AM

"John, where's Jesus?" Andrew had just walked into the room.

John looked up from the scroll he was puzzling over. "Upstairs, I think. Why?"

"Jairus and two other leaders from the Capernaum Synagogue are here, and want to talk to him. They're waiting in the courtyard."

"Oh, okay, I'll go find him." John located Jesus and followed him into the courtyard, where three chiefs of the synagogue were waiting.

Jesus said, "What do you need of me?"

"Teacher," said Jairus, "the centurion Claudius of the Roman garrison here has a servant who is dear to him, who fell from a roof yesterday. He is in terrible pain, and is lying at home paralyzed. The centurion has asked if you would heal his servant. Claudius is worthy to have this done for him, for he loves our nation, and he is the one who paid to have our synagogue built."

"Take me to this man and his servant," said Jesus.

John and Andrew followed Jesus and the synagogue chiefs out the gate. As they walked through the streets, a dozen or so men noticed it was Jesus, and began following them.

When they were not far from the centurion's house, two men came to meet them. One of them said to Jesus, "Lord, our friend Claudius says not to trouble yourself, for he says he is not worthy to have you come under his roof. Because of that he did not come, but he asks you to only say the word, and his servant will be healed."

The other man continued, saying, "Claudius says that he too is a man set under authority with soldiers under him, and he says to one, 'Go,' and he goes, and to another 'Come,' and he comes, and to his servants 'Do this,' and they do it."

When Jesus heard this, he was amazed. He turned to the group following him and said, "I tell you, with no one in Israel have I found such faith."

"I tell you the truth," Jesus continued, "many men and women such as him will come from east and west and recline at table to dine with Abraham, Isaac, and Jacob in the kingdom of God, while the children of Abraham will be thrown into the outer darkness. In that place there will be weeping and gnashing of teeth."

Jesus turned back to the friends of the centurion and said, "Go; it is done for Claudius just as he has believed." [26]

On the way back home, John asked Andrew, "Why do they call him a centurion? I thought centurions were supposed to command a hundred soldiers. The Roman garrison here in Capernaum only has thirty or so`."

Andrew said, "No, a centurion can have any number up to a hundred. And if they need more soldiers in Capernaum, a qualified leader is already in command."

"Oh," he replied.

Later, John learned that the centurion's servant was healed at the very moment that Jesus spoke.

15

CHUZA THE SYRIAN

MONDAY 30 MAY AD 28, 2:00 PM

John and Matt Junior were on the doorsteps of Matthew's house poring over the scroll of Joshua. Sarah was watching and listening while looking after her two youngest brothers, Hebron and Uzziel, who were playing nearby.

"Here it is!" exclaimed John. "Here it is in the scroll, just before Joshua fought Jericho." [27]

"Are you sure?" asked Matt.

"Well, what do you think? Look here, Joshua sees a man with a sword who declares he is the commander of God's heavenly army, and then Joshua falls down before him and worships him."

"You're right about one thing. The man couldn't be an angel, because Joshua wouldn't worship an angel. And if he did, the angel would stop him from doing it."

John said, "Yes, so it's someone higher than an angel, but it's not Yahweh, it's someone in command of Yahweh's army."

Sarah heard John use God's personal name, and moved in closer to peer over John's shoulder. "Oh, I see the Sacred

Name," Sarah said. "Look, it's in there twice!" She leaned over John to point at the two places where the Name was written.

The flower in Sarah's hair brushed against John's cheek, and he was distracted from his chain of thought. John collected himself and traced the words with his finger: "You're right, Sarah. In the first sentence, the man says 'I come now as commander of the army of Yahweh.' Then it says the 'commander of the army of Yahweh' told Joshua to take off his sandals, because he was standing on holy ground."

Sarah said, "Look, in the first place it has 'commander,' 'army,' and the Sacred Name squeezed together like they were all one word. In the second place it has 'commander' and 'army' squeezed together, but the Sacred Name is separated by an empty space. Why is that?"

John was surprised at Sarah's perceptive and highly technical question. "Sarah, I don't really know. Do you know why, Matt?"

Matt said, "In the first spot, the scripture is emphasizing God's mighty power by putting stress on 'commander' and 'army.' In the second spot, it is emphasizing God's holiness by putting stress on the Sacred Name."

Matt continued, "John, I think you may be right. If the ground Joshua was standing on is holy, it's because the man with the sword is holy. Like you said, this could be an appearance on earth of the Great Messiah himself, written in ancient Scripture long before he comes to save Israel and all the peoples."

"Yes," said John, "and if that's true, then the Great Messiah has existed for a long time, and must be the eternal Son of God."

"This would upset quite a few of the teachers of the Law in Jerusalem," said Matt.

Sarah said, "John, why does Jesus switch to the Hebrew language when he calls himself the Son of Man? He always says it in Hebrew, '*ben Adam*,' instead of in Aramaic."

John said, "When he says *ben Adam* he's identifying himself with the first man, Adam, whose only father was God. If he should say it in Aramaic, he would be identifying himself with the 'one like a son of man' in the prophecy of Daniel. That one is the Messiah who comes with the clouds of heaven."

"But isn't Jesus the Messiah?"

"If he calls himself the 'one like a son of man,' they may kill him because he's making himself equal to God."

Then Sarah teased him, "So John, when are you going to open up your own rabbinical school and gather your disciples around you?"

John blushed, and said, "Not me! Your brother's the one who wants to be a teacher of the Law. What about that, Matt? Are you gonna study under one of the scribes in Jerusalem?"

Matt said, "My dad was gonna pay to send me to one of the Jerusalem schools. But none of them would accept me, because I was the son of a tax collector."

"Isn't there any teacher of the Law that'll take you in?"

"Yes, there's Gemariah here in Capernaum. He studied under Nicodemus in Jerusalem. But Nicodemus won't let him start taking in students until he's thirty years old. He has to wait six more years before he can start his own school. Anyway, now I'm a disciple of Jesus. That changes everything. I think Jesus is going to turn all the schools in Jerusalem upside down."

Sarah said, "I saw Gemariah. Hasn't he been following Jesus around listening to him?"

"Yes he has," said John. "I think he might become a disciple."

Just then, someone knocked on the gate, and Sarah went to answer it. Two horses were tied outside, and two men were at the gate, one of them rather richly dressed. John thought he recognized the other man, perhaps from the feast for Jesus that Matthew had held at his house last year.

The richly dressed man asked to see Matthew Senior. Sarah said, "And who should I say is calling on my father?"

"Tell him it is Chuza, the steward of Herod Antipas. He knows me."

John rolled up the scroll, and Matt stood up to greet the visitors. "I will take you to see my father," said Matt.

John said "Matt, what happened?" Chuza and the other man had just mounted their horses outside and were riding away, as Matt was closing the gate.

"Chuza wanted to see his wife Joanna, to get her to return home with his son Michael. He was asking my dad to plead with Jesus for him. He said he was sorry for hitting his wife."

"What did your dad do?"

"He advised Chuza to repent and be baptized," said Matt. "The other man is Perez the tax collector, one of my dad's friends. He was at the feast in our house last year and was baptized in the name of Jesus himself. My dad's gonna see if Jesus wants to meet with Chuza. We're going over to Peter's house now."

"Oh, this should be interesting," said John.

When John and Matt and his father arrived at Peter's house, Joanna's son Michael was in the courtyard and followed them into the house. John went upstairs and told Jesus about the events so far. Jesus said, "Go find Concordia and Joanna, and I will meet with you all downstairs."

When they all assembled, the elder Matthew recounted his conversation with Chuza, ending by saying, "It sounded to me as if Chuza is genuinely sorrowful for striking his wife."

Jesus said, "You are correct, Matthew, but there is an evil spirit involved here. When Chuza becomes angry the spirit will take advantage of him, and he will do wrong again. This demon must be dealt with before Joanna can return to Chuza safely."

Michael said, "There's a spirit living in our house in Tiberias that sometimes moves things around. My dad says it's just a playful spirit, and isn't dangerous. But I'm afraid of it."

Jesus said, "Yes, child, but this foul spirit serves the father of all lies, and has been assigned by the Evil One to deceive your dad and lead him astray."

Jesus continued, "Joanna my daughter, do not tremble, for you and your son will be safe with me until your husband has been completely healed. And Matthew, bring your friend Perez to me. Chuza needs a counselor to deal with this."

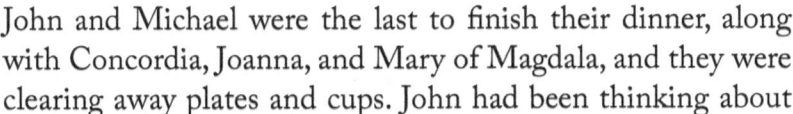

John and Michael were the last to finish their dinner, along with Concordia, Joanna, and Mary of Magdala, and they were clearing away plates and cups. John had been thinking about what Michael had said to Jesus.

"Michael, tell me more about the spirit at your house. Did you see it?"

"No," said Michael. "But once I had a willow hoop leaning against the wall by my bed, and it rolled all by itself into the other room. That was spooky. But my dad told me not to be afraid."

Joanna said, "I saw cupboard doors open and close by themselves, and sometimes I thought I saw a shadow passing, but when I looked again, it wasn't there. It was creepy."

Concordia said, "I wouldn't know what to do about that, before I met Jesus."

Mary of Magdala said, "The first spirit that came to me acted very friendly. She told me she loved me and that no one else would ever love me because of what happened to me. She comforted me a lot, because I was so sad and depressed and lonely and afraid. Then she invited more spirits to come live with me, and they said they loved me too, and they'd never leave me. But they wouldn't let me have any other friends."

"But we love you, Mary," said Concordia.

"Thank you, Concordia. Jesus told me that Father God will always love me and Jesus loves me too. Those spirits were lying to me and holding me captive."

"You're free from them now, Mary," said Joanna. "You never have to worry about them again."

"Yes, Mary," said Concordia, "you've been saved by Jesus and you'll always be safe. I'm so glad you and Joanna are with us."

16

PRAY FOR YOUR ENEMIES

TUESDAY 1 JUNE AD 28, 6:00 AM

John was waiting at the gate when Jesus returned from praying in the hills. On most mornings, Jesus had been gathering the Twelve for a morning teaching in Peter's courtyard, usually attended by some of the other residents at Peter's house. Concordia and Mary the Magdalene were never absent, and today Perez the tax collector was also invited.

In the afternoons, Jesus had been calling all of his disciples together, either for a private teaching at Matthew's house or for a public teaching at the synagogue.

But today seemed different: Jesus had something on his mind. "John, call Peter and your brother and the Zealot. I need to speak to you four."

Disciples were gathering in the courtyard for the morning teaching, but Jesus and the four men were standing in the dining area. Jesus faced Peter, looked him in the eye, and put his finger on Peter's chest: "Simon son of Jonah, have you been praying for the Pharisees and Sadducees who want to destroy me?"

Peter was flustered, and stammered, "Uh—well—uh—no Master, I have not."

Then Jesus turned to James and did the same, saying, "James son of Zebedee, have you been praying for Herod called Antipas, the king of Galilee and Perea?"

James said, "Ah—no, Master, I haven't."

Next, he turned to Simon, and with his finger on his chest, said, "Simon of Hebron, my Zealot, have you been praying for the Romans occupying our land?"

"No, Master, I have not."

Then it was John's turn: "John son of Zebedee, my beloved one, have you been praying for the Herodians, who have been plotting my death?"

John felt Jesus' finger burning at his chest. All he could manage was, "N-no, Master."

"Even so have I noticed," said Jesus. "I have a mission for you four, but you are not spiritually prepared. My Father loves all people, and you also must have loving concern for them. Who knows which of our enemies will repent, and turn, and gain a place in the kingdom of God? My Father knows their hearts, but you do not.

"I want you to prepare yourselves by praying for your enemies each night as you go to sleep and each morning as you awaken. And do not neglect your other prayers as well.

"On the third day, you will be going out as my emissaries into a den of ravening wolves, and there you will fight for the kingdom of God. Take no physical weapons with you, but instead arm yourselves with the spiritual weapons of truth and love. I will provide you with some training, and you will do well."

17

WHO YOU GONNA CALL?

THURSDAY 3 JUNE AD 28, 10:00 AM

"This doesn't look anything like Jerusalem," thought John. "It reminds me of the new Greek section of Bethsaida. Is this what a Roman city is supposed to look like?"

John had never been here before. He was deep inside the newly completed, walled city of Tiberias, built to honor the Roman emperor, Tiberius Caesar. He was following Peter, James, and Simon of Hebron. Perez was leading them to the dignified house of Chuza, the manager in charge of Herod Antipas' personal estates and land holdings.

Yesterday John had watched as Perez and Matthew Senior baptized Chuza in the Sea of Galilee. After that, Chuza had visited with his wife Joanna at Matthew's house, and they agreed that Joanna and Michael would be following Jesus for the time being, before returning home.

At Chuza's gate, Peter took out the vial of olive oil that Jesus had given him and dabbed some on the gateposts, saying,

"May God's peace be upon this house and all who dwell here." Perez knocked and a servant opened the gate for them.

Chuza was there, and Perez said, "Good morning, Chuza. As we discussed, these disciples have been sent by Jesus to rid your house of evil spirits. They would be pleased if you would show them through your house and tell them who uses each room and what takes place there." Perez introduced each of the four to Chuza, and they stepped in through the front door.

John had a cold feeling wash over him. He said, "There are *three* spirits in here somewhere! They've called in reinforcements!"

Peter anointed the doorposts with oil and said, "Foul spirits, in the name of Jesus of Nazareth the Anointed One, I cancel your assignment here. Get out! Go back to where you came from! Satan, you and your minions are banished from this place in the name of Jesus. Depart, and never return!"[28]

The four disciples followed Chuza through all the rooms of the house, with Peter reciting similar words while anointing each doorframe. They came to the last room at the back of the house, where the door was closed. Peter asked Chuza, "What room is this?"

He said, "This is my sleeping room, where I can have my privacy."

Peter opened the door, and three mighty blasts of frigid air washed over the disciples, almost forcing them back. Yet the hair on their heads was undisturbed, as if there had been no wind at all. John said, "Whoa! What was that?"

James looked around the room. He said, "Look! There's a niche in the wall above the bed, and there's a wooden idol sitting in it! Chuza, do you pray to that idol?"

Chuza said, "No, I do not. I pray only to the Most High God, the maker of heaven and earth."

Simon the Zealot said, "Well, it has to go. In fact, it has to be destroyed."

Chuza said, "But that's a precious family heirloom I brought with me when I left Syria. My father and grandfather used to pray to it, but no one here pays any attention to it."

Peter said, "If you permit that idol to remain here, or even to continue to exist, you are permitting Satan to send more evil spirits into your household to wreak destruction upon your life. You must destroy it, or no peace will descend upon you and your family."

Chuza was conflicted. "It's been in my family over a hundred years. Is there no other way?"

James said, "No there is not. For you and your family, this is a seed of destruction."

Chuza asked, "What must I do then?"

Peter said, "You must take it by your own hand and throw it into the kitchen fire. We will stay with you until it is completely consumed by the flames."

Chuza reluctantly picked up the idol from its niche in the wall. John looked at the empty niche, which now looked like it was beckoning to be filled. He turned to Peter and said, "Why don't we leave the vial of olive oil here?"

"Good idea," said Peter. John took the vial from Peter and placed it in the niche.

Peter said, "Chuza, Jesus prayed over this vial and this oil that it might be a sign of the blessing and the love of God for your house. It is not something to be prayed to. It is an outward and visible sign of an inward and spiritual gift to your household."

The five men then went to the kitchen where Chuza threw the idol into the flames of the kitchen fire and they watched it being consumed.

Leaving the house, Peter turned to place his hand on the doorframe once more. Loudly he proclaimed, "By the authority of Jesus of Nazareth, I seal this house against the Evil One in the name of Yahweh our Father, Jesus his only Son, and by the Holy Spirit of God."

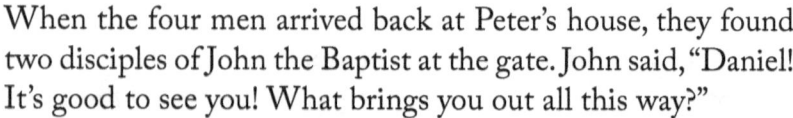

When the four men arrived back at Peter's house, they found two disciples of John the Baptist at the gate. John said, "Daniel! It's good to see you! What brings you out all this way?"

Daniel said, "Hi, John. The Prophet sent the two of us to get him an update on what Jesus is doing and saying, so we've come to pay you a visit. I think you know Linus, here."

John said, "Yes, Linus, I remember you. You were with the Baptist on the day I met Jesus."

Linus said, "I'm looking forward to seeing Jesus again, John."

John said, "Well, this house is kind of full—besides all the men, there are seven women living here. But there's room at Matthew's house, with the rest of Jesus' disciples. I'll take you over and introduce you. You'll enjoy it; and you'll be welcome to attend the teaching Jesus does there most every afternoon."

"Oh, that sounds good," said Daniel.

"And wait'll I tell you what we've been doing today! We've been casting out demons in the name of Jesus!"

18

ON THE ROAD AGAIN

TUESDAY 15 JUNE AD 28, 2:00 PM

John was walking beside Jesus, who was beginning a tour of Galilee with his chosen Twelve. They were spreading the good news about the kingdom of God. Also walking with Jesus were the four women: Concordia, Susanna, Mary of Magdala, and Joanna with her son Michael.

For the first time, John thought, they were well supplied with funds for their road trip. When Chuza had come to visit Joanna, he had given her a gift of a small sack of coins. When she opened it later, she found twelve gold aureus coins, almost a year's salary for a Roman soldier. She told Concordia she didn't need the money and asked her what she should do with it. They decided to give it for the support of Jesus and his disciples, and entrusted the twelve Roman aurei to Judas of Kerioth. Also, Susanna provided money from her inheritance, and several other women believers were supporting Jesus and his mission from their own funds.[29]

Walking behind the Twelve and the Four were the rest of Jesus' disciples. Jesus was releasing them to return to their home towns and spread the good news among their friends and families, following their month of training in Capernaum. Many of them were going south to Jerusalem to celebrate the Feast of Weeks[30] before returning to their homes. Joses son of Alpheus was on his way to serve as a Levite in the temple during the festival.

A robust crowd was traveling along with them, including the two disciples of the Baptist. Most of these were also on their way to the festival, but they were sticking close to Jesus to see what he might do or say. Jesus was traveling south, headed for the village of Nain.

As they drew near to Nain, a column of people was coming out of the wooden town gate toward them. John thought they were coming out to greet Jesus, but it turned out to be a funeral procession on its way to the town cemetery. They were carrying a dead boy on a funeral bier.

Jesus asked the man leading the procession, "What has happened here? Who has died?"

The man said, "This widow of our town has suffered a grievous loss. Her son—her only child—has died, and she does not know what life holds for her now. She will have no one to live with and no one to care for her in her old age."

Jesus saw the woman walking beside the funeral bier, distraught and weeping. He was deeply touched, and drew near to her, saying, "Woman, don't cry."

Then he came up and touched the bier. The bearers stopped, and a hush fell over the crowd. Everyone was watching to see what Jesus might do.

Jesus said, "Young man, I say to you, get up!" The dead boy sat up on the funeral bier and started talking! Jesus helped him down and gave him to his mother. She was utterly astounded, and her tears of grief turned to tears of joy.

A great awe swept through the crowds. Many began shouting, "Praise God!" and "God has visited his people today!"

and "A mighty prophet has risen among us today!" But a small group of Pharisees stood on the outside of the crowd, scowling.

John had tears in his eyes, watching the mother and son cling to each other. Daniel came up to John and said, "That was incredible. Linus and I are leaving you now to go back to the prison and report all these doings to the Prophet."[31]

19

Woes and Comfort

FRIDAY 18 JUNE AD 28, 4:00 PM

Peter, John, and Andrew were sitting on the steps of the small synagogue in Nain when Nathanael appeared, coming in from the town gate. Peter said, "Nate! We've missed you! Where've you been since Tuesday?"

Nathanael said, "Well, did you notice the group of Pharisees spying on us Tuesday?"

"Yes, I saw them," Peter said. "I was keeping an eye on them."

"I thought you would be," said Nathanael. "I was listening to what they were saying to the crowd that day. They were arguing with the people, saying Jesus didn't really raise that young man from the dead, that it was a trick of some sort. They were trying to stop people from calling Jesus a prophet."

Peter asked, "What did you do, follow them?"

"Yup. They didn't seem to recognize I was a disciple of Jesus, so I figured I could do some spying too. I mixed with the crowd going to the festival, and they didn't notice me. Those Pharisees and their friends were mostly from Capernaum and Bethsaida, and one of them was from Chorazin."

John asked, "So what did you learn?"

"I learned they were planning to alert the temple police that Jesus was coming to Jerusalem for the festival. They were hoping the police would arrest Jesus to stop him from teaching. They didn't know Jesus wasn't going to Jerusalem, but was headed for Jezreel instead."

Peter said, "Right! We weren't even planning to stop here in Nain, but the raising of that boy changed everything. Since you've been gone, Jesus has healed more people and we've baptized just about everyone in the town."

Andrew said, "The first night after you left was real turmoil, Nate, 'cause there were so many people here. Last year when we got here after Passover, there were only nine of us. This time it was more like seventy or eighty disciples, plus the crowd behind us. That was more than Nain could handle, and a lot of people had to sleep outside the gates. It's settled down now; most everyone left the next day to hurry to Jerusalem. I think tonight there's gonna be room in the synagogue for everyone."

Peter said, "Yes, Jesus was asked to speak in the synagogue tonight and tomorrow morning, and then we're moving on after that."

Jesus stood up to receive the scroll of Isaiah from the elder of the synagogue. He rolled the heavy scroll open, found the appointed scripture, and began to read:

> This is what the Lord says: "I will expose that righteousness you claim, and those works of which you are so proud. When you cry out for help, these idols of yours will not save you; a puff of air will blow them away! But the one who takes refuge in me will inherit the land, and will take possession of my holy mountain."

> For this is what the high and lofty one says—he who lives forever, whose name is sacred: "I live in a high and lofty place, but I also live with those who are contrite and lowly in spirit. I will lift up the spirit of the lowly, and revive the heart of the contrite. But I will not accuse forever, nor will I always be angry, lest the spirit of man should grow faint before me." [32]

Jesus rolled up the scroll, handed it to the elder, and sat down with John sitting near him. All eyes in the synagogue were on him, as they waited for him to speak.

Jesus began, "Before your eyes this scripture has come to pass. The lowly and humble of Nain have seen a great light, while the high and mighty from the cities of the lake—the ones who claim righteousness and wisdom—have been groping in their blindness.

"Woe to you, Chorazin! Woe to you, Bethsaida! If the mighty works done in you had been done in Tyre and Sidon, they would have repented long ago in sackcloth and ashes. But I tell you, it will be more bearable on the Day of Judgment for Tyre and Sidon than for you.

"And you, Capernaum, will you be exalted to heaven? No, you will be brought down to Hades. If the mighty works done in you had been done in Sodom, it would have remained until this day. But I tell you it will be more tolerable on the Day of Judgment for the land of Sodom than it will be for you."

Jesus looked around the room at the people of Nain and the Twelve and the Four, and declared, "I thank you, Father, Lord of heaven and earth. You have hidden these things from those who think themselves wise and understanding, and have revealed them instead to little children.

"Yes, Father, for this was your gracious will. All things have been given over to me by my Father. No one knows the Father except the Son, and the Son reveals the Father to those whom he chooses—those given to him by the Father."

Jesus stood and raised his arms wide, with a broad smile on his face. He said, "Come to me, all you who labor and are heavily burdened, and I will give you rest. Take my yoke upon your shoulders, and learn from me, for I am gentle and lowly in heart, and you will find rest for your souls. For my yoke is easy, and my burden is light." [33]

The people were astonished by words of such elegance, peace, and comfort.

John felt a wave of peace roll over him. He would sleep well tonight.

20

MESSAGE TO THE BAPTIST

FRIDAY 2 JULY AD 28, 2:00 PM

Thaddeus said, "There's the well!"

"I see it, Tad," said John. "There's supposed to be a second one around here too." Peter had sent John and Thaddeus to fetch water for Jesus and his disciples. They were visiting Afula, a nearby village on a small hill in the midst of the farm-fields, on the fertile soil of the plain of Jezreel. They were carrying empty water jars borrowed from the villagers.

Thaddeus said, "Hey, there's two guys sitting next to the well!"

"Yeah, I think I recognize them." When they got closer, John could see it was Daniel and Linus, two disciples of John the Baptist.

"Hey Daniel," said John, "I thought you guys went back to Fort Machaerus to report to the Baptist in Herod's prison!"

"Yeah, we did," said Daniel. "But as soon as we got there and told the Prophet what happened in Nain, he sent us back here to ask Jesus a question."

Thaddeus said, "Hey, you guys made good time. You must be tired."

"Naw, we're alright," said Linus. "Where's Jesus?"

"He's in the village over there on the hill," said John. "He'll be teaching there tonight. You'll be able to ask him your question then."

Jesus was teaching from the outdoor steps of the tiny synagogue, where people had gathered from the farming villages and hamlets across the plain of Jezreel, called Esdraelon in the Greek. He was healing many people of diseases and plagues and evil spirits, and restoring sight to the blind.

When the last person seeking help had been healed, Jesus said, "Now who is it that has come to me with a question?"

Daniel and Linus stepped forward, and Daniel said, "John the Baptist has sent us to ask you, 'Are you the One who is to come, or shall we look for another?'"

Jesus said, "Go and tell John what you have seen and heard: the blind receive their sight, the lame walk, lepers are cleansed, the deaf hear, the dead are raised up, and the poor have good news preached to them. And blessed is the one who is not offended by me." [34]

As Daniel and Linus left, Jesus asked the crowd, "Now which of you went out into the wilderness to see and hear John the Baptist?"

Many hands were raised. Jesus continued, "And what did you go out into the wilderness to see? A reed shaken by the wind?

The crowd did not answer. "What then did you go out to see? A man dressed in soft clothing? But look, those who dress in splendid clothing and live in luxury are found in the courts of kings, not in the wilderness.

"What then did you go out to see? Perhaps a prophet? Yes, I tell you, and more than a prophet. This is the one about whom it is written, 'Look! I send my messenger before your face, who will prepare your way before you.' [35]

"Truly I say to you, among those born of women there has risen no one greater than John the Baptist. Yet the one who is least in the kingdom of God is greater than he. For the Prophets and the Law prophesied until John, and if you are willing to accept it, he is the Elijah who is to come. Anyone who has ears to hear, let him hear.

"From the first days of John the Baptist until now, the kingdom of God has been forcefully breaking out, and the breaker will take it with force.

"To what then shall I compare the people of this generation, and what are they like? They are like children sitting in the marketplace and calling to their playmates, 'We played the flute for you, and you didn't dance; we sang a funeral song, and you didn't weep.'

"For John the Baptist came eating no bread and drinking no wine, and you say, 'He has a demon.' But the *Son of Man* came eating and drinking, and you say, 'Look at him! A glutton and a drunkard, a friend of tax collectors and sinners!'

"Yet wisdom has been justified by her true children, while those in splendid clothing have stood to the side with their ears stopped up and their eyes covered." [36]

That evening Jesus, the twelve apostles, and the four women followers were gathered together for supper. John was reclining next to Jesus, and said, "Teacher, all the people who received the baptism of John were glad to hear what you said about him tonight, even two tax collectors."

Jesus said, "Yes John, but many Pharisees and teachers of the Law have rejected the Baptist's call for repentance, and by doing so they have rejected the Father's purpose for themselves."

"And teacher," John went on, "please explain to us about the 'breaker.'"

"Yes, John. The prophet Micah tells us that when God gathers the sheep of his pasture there will come a breaker. That is the prophet Elijah, who will break open the gate of the sheepfold to release the flock. Then the king will lead the flock into God's kingdom, with the Father at their head. This is taking place even now, and your eyes have been blessed to see it." [37]

The summer stars were bright overhead. Jesus and John were walking in the cool of the evening before retiring for the night, and John was reflecting on Jesus' lesson from Micah.

John said, "Teacher, I was thinking that if Elijah is the breaker that releases the flock of God, then the king who leads them out must be the Messiah we are expecting."

"You have judged correctly, John. The Anointed One leads his people to the kingdom."

"Back in Capernaum Matt and I were wrestling with the story of Joshua, where he meets the captain of the armies of God. If the captain of God's army led his people into the Promised Land, then maybe he's the same person as the Messiah who leads them into the kingdom."

"Ah, you have been wrestling indeed—not just with stories, John, but you have been wrestling with God."

"Wow. I didn't think of it that way."

"When we get back to Capernaum, John, put away the scroll of Joshua and find my scroll of the first book of Moses.[38] Then you and Matt can wrestle with the one who wrestled with Jacob. That will lead you deeper into even more questions."

21

A Woman Anointing

THURSDAY 8 JULY AD 28, 7:00 AM

John, Andrew, Philip, Thaddeus, Michael, Judas, and the Zealot were sightseeing. They were climbing up an almost two hundred foot high mound on the south side of the Plain of Jezreel. Michael asked, "What is this place, anyway?"

John said, "This is the Hill of Megiddo, the *'Har-Mageddon.'* Jesus showed me a hilltop in Nazareth where you could look all the way across the plain of Jezreel and see this mound."

Philip said, "There's an old fortress at the top. Many wars have been fought here. King Josiah of Judah, the righteous one, was killed here by the enemies of God."

"Yes," said John, "and one day the enemies of God will gather again around the *Har-Mageddon* to make war against his righteous ones." [39]

Andrew and Philip gave John a strange look. This was not the first time they had heard John prophesy about the future.

Judas of Kerioth said, "Those enemies won't have a chance, if the Messiah is leading the mighty forces of God. I can't wait for that to happen."

Arriving at the top, they saw a Pharisee and his young son walking around the edge and looking at the expansive view. Arriving at where the disciples were standing, he stopped to talk to them. He asked, "Are you some of the disciples of Jesus of Nazareth?"

Simon the Zealot said, "Yes we are. I am Simon of Hebron. Why do you ask?"

"Ah, I am Simon also. They call me Simon the Pharisee of Megiddo, because I like to walk up here to pray. I have heard of the controversy Jesus of Nazareth has been creating by healing people on the Sabbath. A few of us Pharisees believe he is not far wrong in what he teaches."

The Zealot said, "Oh really? I haven't yet heard a Pharisee defending Jesus."

John thought to himself, *"That's because you haven't heard Nicodemus, one of the rulers of Jerusalem, talk with Jesus."*

"Yes," said the Pharisee, "But I believe they have forgotten the lesson we learned more than 160 years ago when the enemies of God tried to wipe out our religion. At least a thousand righteous men, women, and children were slaughtered when they refused to defend themselves on the Sabbath. As soon as our hero Mattathias heard of that, they decided that never again would Jews fail to defend themselves on the Sabbath."[40]

Thaddeus said, "So that's why this rule is still in place today?"

"Yes. It does not honor the Sabbath if you make yourself into your own enemy because of it.[41] In the same way, shouldn't a sick person who sees he can be made well on the Sabbath take that chance when he can? The Sabbath is for life, and not for death."

"You have spoken well," said the Zealot. "If you heard the rest of the teachings of our master, you might find them also to be wise."

"Yes, I would like to hear him. Tell your master that he and his friends are invited for dinner tonight, and I will invite some of my friends also. I live in a village about a mile south of here." The disciples walked down the hill with the Pharisee and his son, and followed them toward his house to be shown the way. When a woman approached from the other direction, the Pharisee scowled and walked to the far side of the road to avoid her, as if she were carrying a disease.

John thought that was peculiar. "Simon," he asked, "why did you avoid that woman? Is she carrying a foul disease?"

He said, "No, child. That was the most notorious sinner around here. She claims to be a seamstress, but she lives all by herself, and allows single male travelers to lodge with her as they pass through these parts."

John didn't like his answer very much, and he disliked being called a child even more. Only Jesus called him that, and Jesus used it as a term of affection. Once they had seen the Pharisee's house, the disciples turned back to the place where they were lodging with Jesus.

Judas of Kerioth said, "I don't trust that guy. I think he made all that up, just so he could get a chance to spy on us and find out what we're doing and what our plans are."

The Zealot said, "You might be right, Judas, but we'll let Jesus make that decision."

Coming in the door, they were startled to find the "sinner" woman talking with Jesus. They told Jesus about the invitation, and he not only accepted it, but also invited the woman to come along with them. Simon and Judas went back to inform Simon the Pharisee of Jesus' acceptance.

Jesus went into the Pharisee's house and reclined at the table with John near him. The sinner woman had brought an alabaster flask of ointment, and at Jesus' feet she wept and began to wet his feet with her tears. She wiped them with the hair of her head and kissed his feet and anointed them with the ointment. When the Pharisee saw this, he winced in revulsion.

Jesus said, "Simon, I have something to say to you."

And he said, "Say it, teacher."

"A certain moneylender had two debtors. One owed five hundred denarii, and the other fifty. When they could not pay, he cancelled the debt of both. Now which one will love him more?"

Simon said, "The one, I suppose, for whom he cancelled the larger debt."

Jesus said, "You have judged rightly." Then turning toward the woman he said to Simon, "Do you see this woman? I entered your house and you gave me no water for my feet, but she has wet my feet with her tears and wiped them with her hair. You gave me no kiss, but from the time she came in she has not ceased to kiss my feet. You did not anoint my head with oil, but she has anointed my feet with ointment. Therefore I tell you, her sins, which are many, are forgiven—for she loved much. But the one who is forgiven little, loves little."

And Jesus said to the woman, "Your sins are forgiven you."

Simon's friends at table with him looked shocked at this saying.

But Jesus said again to the woman, "Your faith has saved you; go in peace." [42]

22

The Witch of Endor

WEDNESDAY 21 JULY AD 28, 10:00 AM

Jesus and his disciples were on their way back north to Capernaum, leaving the Jezreel valley where Jesus had been teaching at the small farming villages on the plain. They were being followed by a group of lakeside residents who had sought them out after returning from the Feast of Weeks at Jerusalem.

John noticed some familiar faces, and found his way over to Nathanael's side. He said, "Nate, aren't those three guys over there the Pharisees you were spying on?"

"Yeah John," he said, "I'm afraid my secret is out. You should've seen the face of one when he spotted me. I imagine they got sent here by the Jerusalem Pharisees to spy on Jesus some more."

"Well I dunno what they hope to gain. Jesus is still going to be Jesus. We'll see what they do when we get to Endor. One of the farmers invited us to have a snack there."

"Yeah, that'll be interesting. I heard of an old woman there who pretends to be the Witch of Endor. She tells fortunes for a living, and the landowner takes half her earnings in exchange for his protection. She's prob'ly a fake, just trying to make money from the Scripture story about the real Witch of Endor, the one who prophesied for King Saul." [43]

As they approached Endor a couple hours after noonday, a group of ten locals were waiting for them on the road. Jesus called out loudly to them, "Step forward, spirit! Your time for deceiving the children of Abraham is at an end!"

An old woman stepped forward, and said, "What do you want with me? I know who you are: the Holy One of God!"

"Silence! Spirit, come forth from this woman, and depart into the wilderness," said Jesus.

The woman stiffened, then slowly a look of peace and joy came over her face. She said "I'm free! I'm free!" Then suddenly her face took on a look of confusion. "But… But… What will I do now to support myself? And who will protect me when the landlord finds out I can't tell fortunes anymore?"

Jesus said to her, "Take care, woman, and keep free from sin. For when an unclean spirit has gone from someone, it passes through desolate places looking for rest, but doesn't find any. Then it says, 'I'll go back to the house I came from.' When it gets there, it finds the house vacant and swept clean, with everything in order. Then it goes to find seven other spirits more evil than itself, and they enter and dwell there. And the last condition of that person will be worse than the first."

As Jesus and his disciples passed on from there, two blind men from the group of locals followed them, crying aloud, "Have mercy on us, son of David." They arrived at the house of the farmer, who invited them up an outdoor stairway to a room large enough for Jesus and the disciples.

The blind men groped their way up the stairs also and said again, "Have mercy on us, son of David."

Jesus came to the door and said to them, "Do you believe I am able to heal you?"

They said to him, "Yes, Lord."

Then he touched their eyelids, saying, "According to your faith be it done to you," and their eyes were opened and they could see.

Jesus sternly warned them, "See that no one knows about this." But they had hardly got down the stairs before they began spreading Jesus' fame throughout that district.

Lunch was not a normal meal for John and his fisher friends. If they were blessed they might have a crust of bread tucked away in a pocket, and a swallow of water. But today the Twelve and the Four were fed well, with fresh vegetables and succulent fruits from the farmer's garden.

When they left the house the lake-dwellers' group was outside waiting, along with the three Pharisees. As they were departing, the villagers brought a man to Jesus who had been oppressed by a foul spirit for many years. He had been unable to speak a word for all those years.

After Jesus cast out the spirit, the man began to speak. The villagers were astonished. They said, "Nothing like this been seen in Israel!" and, "Can this be the son of David?"

But one of the Pharisees said, "It's only by the power of the prince of demons that this man can cast out demons."

Another one said, "Yes, this man casts out demons by Beelzebub, the Philistine's Lord of the Flies and prince of the house of Satan."

The third one said, "Not only that, but he himself is owned by Beelzebub!" The three Pharisees grinned at each other; they were quite proud of their collective putdown.

But Jesus called the Pharisees to himself and said to them, "How can Satan cast out Satan? If a kingdom is divided against itself, that kingdom cannot stand. If Satan casts out Satan, he is divided against himself. How then will his kingdom survive? You say I cast out demons by Beelzebub. If I cast out demons by Beelzebub, by whom do your own exorcists cast them out?

"But beware, for if it is by Holy Spirit that I cast out demons, then the kingdom of God has come upon you. Therefore I warn you, whoever rejects the *Son of Man* can be forgiven in this age, but whoever rejects the Holy Spirit will not have forgiveness, either in this age or in the age to come.

"Satan is strong, is he not? How can someone enter a strong man's house and plunder his goods, unless he first binds the strong man? When a strong man, fully armed, guards his own house, his goods are safe. But when one who is stronger than he attacks him and overcomes him, he takes away the defenses in which he trusted and divides his spoils. Therefore today you have seen one who is stronger than Satan plunder Satan's house." [44]

The three Pharisees drew off by themselves, and could be heard muttering, "This man is a raving lunatic, and needs to be restrained." [45]

23

BACK TO THE LAKE

SUNDAY 25 JULY AD 28, 2:00 PM

John felt refreshed. On the Sabbath they had spent the day resting in the pools of the Hammath hot springs. On the day before, when they had turned in on the path to the springs, the crowd with them had continued north toward Tiberias and Capernaum. The three Pharisees stopped at the springs, but they kept to themselves. Joanna and Michael continued on to their home in Tiberias, and Susanna returned to her home in nearby Sennabris.

Now they were turning up the street that led to Perpetua's house, and beyond that to Matthew's house. But the street was full of people! Word had spread that Jesus was coming home, and a crowd had gathered. Some were there to be healed, but most of them just wanted to see him and perhaps touch him, or at least have Jesus' shadow fall on them.

Jesus was at the back of his group, and looked weary. He turned to John and said, "Many of these have come from afar with open ears to hear my words. I must teach tomorrow. Have Peter prepare a boat in case the crowd presses in too much."

Peter and Big James and Simon and Judas—and even Concordia—struggled to create a corridor through the crowd so that Jesus could reach Perpetua's gate. Finally they got inside, while Matthew and Matt continued up the street to their own house. Perpetua and Mina greeted the disciples.

Concordia said, "Mom, where's Jesus' mother?"

"Oh, she left the week before last to visit her daughters and grandchildren in Sepphoris. And this week she's visiting her sons and grandchildren in Nazareth," said Perpetua. "Her son Joseph came here to visit and he's travelling with her to help her."

Mina said, "Come on all of you, come sit down and eat! The food's all ready. Since the day before Sabbath, the whole city has known you'd be here today."

Jesus retired upstairs with a plate, and the disciples were reclining at table when there was a loud knocking at the gate. Mina went to answer it, and Simon went with her as backup in case the crowd tried to intrude. They returned with Joses son of Alpheus in tow.

Little James said, "Brother! What are you doing here? I didn't expect you!"

Joses said, "The high priests and elders in Jerusalem have been hatching another plot to get to Jesus. I came as quickly as I could. Actually, there've been several plots developing."

"Oh, tell us!"

Joses said, "In the temple I was talking with a priest I know who's close to the inner circle. The first thing I learned was that two men from Gibeah had come to accuse Jesus of breaking the Law by eating blood. But the priests arranged to hear their testimonies separately. The first one said that Jesus had been giving his blood to his disciples and making them drink it."

Little James said, "If that was true, they could have him punished severely. But of course, nothing like that has happened at all."

"So I figured. But the second witness said that Jesus ordered his body to be cut up and his blood collected, and then his disciples would eat and drink of it. Since their testimonies didn't agree, the Supreme Council had no way to file a charge against him."

John said, "Jesus did say something about blood to me and Andrew. But I didn't understand what he meant, and neither of us had the nerve to ask him about it."

Joses said, "But then the elders came up with another scheme."

Nathanael said, "What was that, Joses?"

"They said only a crazy man would talk like that. Since Jesus was crazy, his family would have to confine him for the protection of the people. And since James the Just is head of the family, they decided to send a delegation to him to demand that he restrain his lunatic brother."

"Oh, no," said Nathanael. "When the high priests' men get to James the Just, he'll have no choice except to start an investigation to find out if his brother is really off his rocker."

"Yes," said Perpetua, "and since James is a fair and just man, he'll bring his brothers and his mother along with him and form a family council to help him with the decision."

"And there's one more thing," said Joses.

"Oh, shoot," said Andrew. "What else is the Supreme Council dreaming up?"

"Well, the council's not all in agreement. A few of them are sympathetic to Jesus, and they're restraining the council from doing anything rash. But the majority answered back, 'Unless this Jesus brings us a mighty sign from heaven, we do not have to believe.'"

"The signs that Jesus already brought look mighty to me," said Andrew, "but some of the Pharisees say it's all trickery. And a few people believe them."

Mealtime was almost over when they heard another loud knock at the gate. Again Mina and Simon went out to answer, and this time they brought back Matthew, followed by his son Matt. "More problems," said Matthew. "My wife Paula says that both the mayor and the Roman centurion are getting complaints from the town merchants about the crowds in the streets. They're calling it a public nuisance. There's even a crowd around my house that thinks I'm hiding Jesus inside. We'll have to do something different."

John said, "Jesus wants to teach tomorrow at the lakeside. He wants Peter to have a boat on standby that he can use in case the crowd presses in too much."

Matthew said, "If we do that right in front of the city the crowds will block the main highway, and we'll still have the complaints. Where can we go?"

Peter said, "Okay, let's plan this right now. How about we set up south of the city where the highway leaves the beach and jogs inland? Andrew and Philip, you two go get my boat tomorrow and make it ready. Simon and Judas, why don't you help them manage the boat offshore from the teaching spot?

"Big James and I will stay by Jesus' side as bodyguards. John, you better stick close too, in case Jesus wants something. Matthew and Thomas, you could help us out with security near Jesus. If he starts healing people, we may have to get them into a line to wait their turn."

Nathanael said, "We need people on the outside of the crowd to watch for troublemakers, too."

"Right, Nate. Little James, how about you and Tad working with Nate to be our eyes and ears around the perimeter?"

"That sounds fine," said Little James. "Tad can be our messenger from the outside to you guys inside. He's good at slipping through crowds. There are rewards for being small."

Peter said, "Okay, we'll need some help with the women in the crowd also. Concordia and Magdalena, you should stick close to Jesus when he's healing, in case any women are overcome or need attention.

Philip said, "As the day goes on, there'll be people who want to be baptized. We should be ready for that."

"You're right, Philip," said Peter. "Why don't you and Joses set up a baptism site near the northern edge of the crowd. And if Susanna and Joanna show up, they can help with the women. More of us can come to help baptize as the crowd winds down. Now, have we left anything out?"

Matthew said, "It sounds thorough to me. If the crowd stays manageable, I can sit and take notes of what Jesus is saying. I'm trying to keep a record of everything he teaches. But let's sleep on it and have a quick council in the morning in case we think of anything else."

"We can meet here an hour before dawn. Let's do this!"

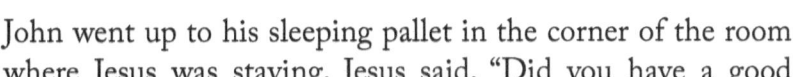

John went up to his sleeping pallet in the corner of the room where Jesus was staying. Jesus said, "Did you have a good council with my disciples?"

"Yes," said John. "Peter sort of took charge and set everything up. We're going to bring his boat south to where the road jogs inland."

"Peter is a good leader when he lets the Father set aside his fears," said Jesus.

24

Parable instead of a sign

MONDAY 26 JULY AD 28, 5:00 AM

Mina and Perpetua had put special effort into the early morning meal. For each person there were two biscuits, two boiled eggs, a cup of steaming tea from India, a piece of cheese, and a piece of fruit. More food was stacked up in the center of the table. John was enjoying the meal.

Peter and Matthew were the last to come in; they had been conferring in the courtyard. Peter said, "Well, does anyone have more thoughts about today?"

Simon the Zealot said, "Yes. There are disciples in Capernaum and the nearby towns that will surely show up to hear Jesus. We should be ready to send them where they can help the most."

"Good idea," said Matthew.

John said, "I was thinking if the crowd is too big, Jesus might want to teach from the boat. And it'd be good to have disciples at the shoreline in case anyone tried wading in to reach him."

"Good idea, John," said Peter. "Anything else?"

Nathanael said, "The rumor on the streets is that Jesus is going to show Galilee a powerful sign from heaven today. I think the Pharisees that've been dogging us started that rumor, but it's been spreading like wildfire in Capernaum and the towns around us. We'll prob'ly get lots of sightseers today trying to get close to Jesus."

"All the more reason to keep a tight circle around the Teacher today," said Big James.

Nothing else was added by the Twelve, who were eating rather than talking.

At two hours after sunrise, more than a hundred people who had followed Jesus to the beach were milling about. Jesus asked for his scroll of Isaiah, and John took Tad with him to run to the house and bring it back. He and Tad weaved back through the crowd to reach Jesus.

Jesus motioned for everyone to sit. Then he rolled open the scroll and found what he had in mind. The crowd grew silent, and he began to read. "Listen to the words of the prophet Isaiah:

> Here is my servant whom I uphold,
>   my chosen one in whom I delight.
> I will put my Spirit on him,
>   and he will bring justice to the nations.
> He will not shout or cry out,
>   or raise his voice in the city streets.
> A bruised reed he will not break,
>   and a smoldering wick he will not snuff out.
> In faithfulness he will bring forth justice;
>   he will not falter nor be discouraged
>   until he establishes justice on the earth.
> In his name the nations will put their hope.[46]

Jesus handed the scroll to John and sat down with the disciples around him. He continued, "Even so Isaiah has foreseen this day: you will not hear the *Son of Man* shouting in the city streets, nor will you see him bringing down destruction. Nevertheless, the *Son of Man* brings salvation for Israel and the nations, and peace between men on earth and our Father in heaven."

The three Pharisees had been joined by more Pharisees and teachers of the Law from the local area. They had worked their way to the front of the crowd and were sitting near the disciples. One of them said, "Teacher, we want to see a sign from you."

The crowd rustled in anticipation. But armed with the news that Nathanael brought, John knew their request was not sincere.

But Jesus said to them, "This is an evil and adulterous generation! It looks for a powerful sign from heaven, but no sign will be given to it except the sign of the prophet Jonah.

"For just as Jonah spent three days in the belly of the great fish, so will the *Son of Man* spend three days in the belly of the earth. Just as Jonah was a sign to the people of Nineveh, so will the *Son of Man* become a sign to this generation.

"The men of Nineveh will rise up at the judgment along with this generation and they will condemn it, for they repented at the preaching of Jonah. But look, something greater than Jonah is here before you! [47]

"The Queen of the South will rise up on the Day of Judgment with the men and women of this generation and she will condemn them. She came from the ends of the earth to hear the wisdom of King Solomon.[48] But look, something greater than Solomon is here before you!" [49]

As Jesus taught, people continued to arrive. By four hours after sunrise, several hundred were sitting around him, with several hundred more standing around the seated people. Outside the standing crowd, even more were milling about. John spotted Tad working his way forward through the seated people, evidently bringing a message.

But before Thaddeus got near, the people began murmuring. While Jesus was still teaching, some of the crowd near him said, "Teacher, your mother and your brothers are standing on the outside, wanting to see you."

But Jesus replied, "Who is my mother, and who are my brothers?" Stretching his hand toward his disciples, he said, "Here are my mother and my brothers! I tell you the truth, whoever does the will of my Father in heaven is my brother and sister and mother. They are the ones who hear the word of God and actually do it." [50]

People were still arriving from town after town, and the crowd grew even larger and started becoming restless. The seated people began to stand up so they wouldn't be trampled. Peter called out, "Andrew! Philip! Bring the boat!"

Jesus and John climbed into the boat, while James, Matthew, and Thomas stood along with Peter at the shoreline. And the whole crowd stood on the beach beside the sea.

Seated in the boat, Jesus signaled for calm, and waited for the crowd to become quiet. Then he called out, "Who has ears to hear? Listen! I have a parable for you!

"A sower went out to sow his seed. And as he sowed, some seed fell along the path and was trampled underfoot, and the birds of the air came and devoured it.

"Other seed fell on rocky ground, and right away it sprang up, but it had no depth of soil. As it grew up, the sun rose and it was scorched. Since it had no root, it withered away, for it had no moisture.

"Other seed fell among thorns, and the thorns grew with it and choked it. Although it grew up, it did not yield any grain.

"But some seed fell into good soil and produced grain. It grew up and increased, yielding thirty times as much grain, or sixty times, or a hundred. He who has ears to hear, let him hear." [51]

Jesus continued teaching them many things, but he taught only with parables.

The sun had been down an hour before they worked their way back to Perpetua's house. Mary the mother of Jesus was there, along with Concordia, Susanna, Joanna, and the Magdalene. They had helped Perpetua and Mina prepare an evening meal.

John and Tad were the first to arrive. John said, "Mother Mary! I'm sorry you couldn't get through the crowd! Are Jesus' brothers here?"

"No, John, they're on their way back to Nazareth. One of the high priests came to James this week saying that Jesus had been accused before the Supreme Council of being completely out of his mind. James had no choice but to gather the family together to investigate. But my boys heard all they needed to hear today from Jesus. That accusation against him was pure nonsense."

Jesus came in the room looking upbeat and vigorous, much like the Baptist looked after a full day of his work. John expected Jesus to be entirely worn out, but then he remembered something Jesus had once said: "My food is to do the will of the one who sent me, and to carry out his work."

The Twelve and the Four and Matt Junior gathered around the table to eat. Beon and Bohan were also there, along with local teacher Gemariah. Eating with them were disciples Tobias from Capernaum, Perez from Tiberias, Matthias from

Cana, Joses from Ephraim, Simon called the Leper all the way from Bethany, and Joseph *bar* Sabbas from even farther away in Hebron. Simon the Leper had been cleansed from his skin disease by Jesus when he was in Bethany near Jerusalem.

Joseph *bar* Sabbas said, "I wonder how many were in the crowd today?"

Nathanael said, "By my count, we had right around a thousand people. But we only baptized a hundred of them. Like Jesus says, a lot of those folk had ears, but heard nothing."

John said, "Teacher, why did you speak to the people today in parables?"

Jesus answered, "To you it has been given to know the secrets of the kingdom of God. But for others they are told in parables, so that 'seeing they may not see, and hearing they may not understand.'[52]

"For in them Isaiah's prophecy is being fulfilled, where it says to tell the people,

> Keep on hearing, but don't understand;
> keep on seeing, but don't take it in.

"For the Father says,

> Make the hearts of this people unfeeling,
> and their ears indifferent,
> and their eyes glazed over;
>
> Otherwise they might see with their eyes,
> and hear with their ears,
> and understand with their hearts,
> and turn to me and be healed.[53]

"But blessed are your eyes, for they see, and your ears, for they hear. In truth I tell you, many prophets, and many men who truly kept the Law, yearned to see what you see, and hear what you hear, but they neither saw nor heard."

Quiet settled over the room as these words sunk in. Then Thaddeus said, "Teacher, please tell us the meaning of the parable of the sower."

"Don't you understand this parable? Then how are you going to understand any parable? Listen:

"The sower sows the word of God. For those who receive the word along the path, Satan comes promptly and takes away the word that was sown in them. The ones on rocky ground receive the word instantly with joy. But they have no root in themselves, and when trials arise because of the word, at once they fall away.

"Those among thorns hear the word and take it in, but the cares of this world and the pursuit of gain enters their hearts and chokes the word, and their fruit does not mature. But those on good soil are the ones who hear the word and accept it and do it. They keep it in a good heart and bear fruit thirtyfold or sixtyfold or a hundredfold." [54]

Jesus continued, "But not all those with open ears got a chance to hear me today. We will go out again tomorrow, but not so early in the morning. Rest well tonight, my friends."

25

WEEDS AND NETS

TUESDAY 27 JULY AD 28, 10:00 AM

Jesus was in the boat again, but John was onshore with Tad and Matt and Michael. Tad said, "There's not so many people today."

"About half, I think," said Matt. "About 500 people."

"It makes me think about the parable Jesus told." Said John, "The ones missing today were here yesterday, but they didn't hear him, because they were just looking for a spectacular sign from heaven."

"That's sad," said Michael. "Jesus can save them from the things they're doing wrong."

Matt said, "I think the problem is that they don't care what they're doing wrong."

"Mmm, yeah," said John.

Jesus motioned from the boat for the crowd to settle down. Then he lifted his voice and said, "The kingdom of God is at hand! Repent, and be baptized as a token of your repentance. Believe the good news! Make ready for the coming of our God. Become ready to stand before him to make an account of yourself."

"Tell me, what is the kingdom of God like? To what can it be compared?"

The crowd was silent.

Jesus continued, "The kingdom of God can be compared to a man who sowed good wheat seed in his field. But while his men were sleeping, his enemy came and scattered weed seeds among the wheat and then slipped away. When the plants came up and began to develop grain, the weeds also appeared.

"So the servants of the master of the house came and said to him, 'Master, didn't you give us good seed to sow in your field? Why then does it have weeds?'

"He said to them, 'My enemy has done this.'

"So the servants said, 'Do you want us to go gather the weeds?'

"He replied, 'No, for in gathering the weeds you may root up the wheat along with them. Let them both grow up together until the harvest. At harvest time I will tell the reapers to gather the weeds first and bind them in bundles to be burned, and then they will gather the wheat into my barn.'

"So pay attention! For the kingdom of God is like a net that was thrown into the sea and gathered fish of every kind. When it was full, men drew it ashore and sat down and sorted the good into the containers prepared for them, but threw away all the bad."

That evening, Jesus and the disciples were at home around the table for an evening meal.

James the Levite said, "We baptized almost 50 people today."

John said, "That's not a lot, for the size of the crowd. But it's like yesterday, when we had a thousand people. They're not hearing the parables. Maybe they don't want to hear."

Michael said, "Teacher, please tell us about the wheat and the weeds."

Jesus said, "The one who sows the wheat seed is the *Son of Man*. The field is the world, and the good seed represents the sons of the kingdom. The weeds are the sons of the evil one, and the enemy who sowed them is the Devil.

"The harvest is the end of the age, and the reapers are angels. Just as the weeds are gathered and burned with fire, so will it be at the end of the age. The *Son of Man* will send his angels, and they will gather out of his kingdom all causes of sin and all lawbreakers, and throw them into the fiery furnace. In that place they will weep and gnash their teeth. Then the righteous will shine like the sun in the kingdom of their Father."

Thaddeus said, "And the same with the parable of the net?"

"Yes. So it will be at the end of the age. The angels will come out and gather every sort of mankind. Then the judge will separate the evil from the righteous and throw them into the fiery furnace. But the righteous will be taken to the dwellings that have been prepared for them. [55]

"He who has ears, let him hear."

26

SEEDS AND LEAVEN

TUESDAY 10 AUGUST AD 28, 10:00 AM

On the first day of the Jewish month of Av, Jesus was teaching in the Capernaum synagogue. As he stood up, John gave him the scroll he had chosen. Jesus unrolled it and said, "Listen to what was written by Ezekiel! The Father says:

> I myself will take a tender young twig from the top of a lofty cedar, and I will plant it on the top of the highest mountain in Israel. It will become a majestic cedar, sending forth branches and bearing fruit. Every kind of bird will nest in it, and find shelter in the shade of its boughs. And all the trees of the field will know that I am the Lord, who brings down the tall tree and raises up the lowly. It is I who wither the green tree and give life to the dead. I am the Lord; I have spoken, and I will do it." [56]

Jesus gave the scroll back to John and sat down. He said, "To what can we compare the kingdom of God? What parable shall we use for it? The kingdom of God is like a grain of mustard that a man planted in his garden. It's the smallest of seeds, yet when it's planted it grows up and becomes taller than all the other plants in the garden. It puts out branches so that the birds of the sky can make nests in its shade." [57]

Jesus went on, "Here's another way to think of the kingdom. It's like a man who scatters seed on the ground. Then he goes to bed and rises up, night and day, night and day. But the seed sprouts and begins to grow, and he does not know how. The earth produces by itself first the blade, then the ear, then the full grain in the ear. But when the grain is ripe, right away the man puts in the sickle, because the harvest has come." [58]

Jesus looked around the room, which was filled with the people of Capernaum, and only two strangers from out of town. He said, "Then to what shall I compare the kingdom of God? The kingdom of God is like a bit of yeast that a woman put into a bushel of flour, and she waited, and all of the dough became ready to bake." [59]

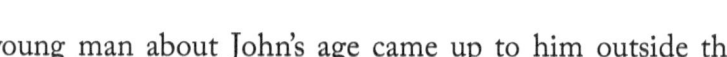

A young man about John's age came up to him outside the synagogue. He said, "Are you one of the disciples of Jesus?"

"Yes, I'm John son of Zebedee."

"I'm Ananias of Damascus. I'm here with my father Anan, and we heard Jesus teaching today. We've come all the way from Damascus so we can be baptized."

John said, "Oh! How did you hear about Jesus?"

"Travelers from the caravans came through last year telling us about John the Baptist. The Baptist was preaching repentance, and warning of the arrival of the Anointed One of God. Then we heard that John was arrested, and that the Anointed One himself rose up to preach the coming of the kingdom of God. Today we heard him teach in the synagogue."

That's amazing," said John. "I didn't know that news of Jesus had travelled so far. There's a lot of Jews in Damascus, aren't there?"

"Yes, more than I can count, and some really big synagogues. But ten of us are forming a new group, the Synagogue of the Anointed One. We want to be followers of Jesus. But how can we become baptized?"

"If you truly believe in Jesus, that's easy," said John. "Just follow me. I'll get a couple of the disciples and we can go down to the lake."

"But what about the rest of our synagogue in Damascus? Do they have to travel here?"

"What you can do is stay with us for a while and get trained as disciples of Jesus. Then you can go back to Damascus and baptize the others."

"Oh, good! Besides the ten of us, there are more who are interested in joining once things get started. Our synagogue should grow to fifty or so pretty quickly."

"Wow," said John. "This is like the parables that Jesus was teaching today."

Perpetua's house and courtyard were full to the brim with guests for dinner. She had invited Matthew and his whole family to come over, along with all the disciples in Capernaum and Magdala, and even Perez from Tiberias. The smell of roasted goat filled the air.

John, Andrew, and Matt had just returned from the lake with Ananias and his father, and John introduced the two them to some of the other disciples. Anan began conversing with Matthew while Ananias, Matt, and John joined the younger group in the courtyard.

Sarah was there, along with her younger brothers. She said, "John! Where have you been? You haven't been over to our house to visit for the longest time!"

John felt embarrassed. "Well, I just got back from a week at home in Bethsaida. But I've been thinking of coming over. I have another scripture I want to study with Matt."

John composed himself and remembered Ananias was standing there beside him. John said, "Oh! Sarah, this is Ananias from Damascus. He and his dad travelled all the way here just to hear Jesus. Ananias, this is Sarah, daughter of Matthew."

Ananias said, "Pleased to meet you, Sarah. Are you studying Scripture with John and your brother?"

"Sort of," said Sarah with a twinkle in her eye. "Mostly I'm just listening in and asking them questions they can't answer."

27

Scripture and Feasting

WEDNESDAY 18 AUGUST AD 28, 12:00 NOON

John was sitting in a corner of Matthew's courtyard with Matt on his right and Sarah on his left. He was rolling open Jesus' scroll of the first book of Moses. "Here it is," John said. "It says the patriarch Jacob 'was left alone, and a man wrestled with him until daybreak.'" [60]

Matt said, "This is when Jacob received his new name, Israel. So now all of us are called Israelites."

"But where did this wrestler come from?" said Sarah.

"We don't know," said Matt. "It doesn't say."

"Whoever he was, Jacob wasn't going to let him go until he got a blessing from him" said John.

"So a name that means 'Wrestles with God' must be a blessing then," said Sarah.

"It beats being ignored by God," said John. "God cares about us. We all wrestle with God."

Matt said, "And then Jacob said he had seen God face to face, and lived to tell it."

"And that's how Jacob learned who the man was, from the name he got?" said Sarah.

"Sure," said Matt. "All the time he was wrestling, he thought it was just a man."

Sarah said, "But which was he, a man, or God?"

Matt said, "That's the real question. Moses says he was a man. Moses says he was God. Since Moses doesn't lie, he must have been both man and God."

"Good point," said John. "And the person that fits that best is the 'one like a son of man', who 'comes with the clouds of heaven.'"

"The Great Messiah," said Sarah.

"Yes," said John.

It was only two hours after noon, but the guests for dinner were already starting to arrive at Matthew's. Today was the "fast of the fourth month," when Jews would refrain from eating. But the followers of Jesus didn't fast, for he had said, "How can the guests of the bridegroom fast while the bridegroom is with them?" [61]

So Matthew had declared a feast and invited anyone who was a follower of Jesus to come. Some of the first arrivals included street beggars, men who had been punished as criminals, and ex-prostitutes who had served the Roman garrison.

John and Matt were taking a turn monitoring the gate to let people in. Nathanael and Philip arrived, and John said, "Hey, Nate, what's up?"

"The synagogue chiefs are displeased, as usual," said Nate, "along with the Pharisees assigned to check on Jesus. They say we're breaking the tradition of the elders by not fasting today. Sounds like something Jesus would dream up."

Matt said, "My mom wanted to throw a thanksgiving feast for Jesus' followers. But it was Jesus who suggested holding it today. He said Zechariah's prophecy will be coming true."

Philip said, "What prophecy was that?"

"I looked it up," said Matt. "It says,

> The fast of the fourth month, and the fifth and seventh and tenth month are ended. These will become days of joy, gladness, and happy feasts for my people. Therefore love truth and peace.
>
> People from all the nations will come to Jerusalem to ask the Most High God for his blessing and mercy. In those times ten men from ten nations will clutch hold of the garment of one Jew, saying, 'Let me be your friend, for we know God is with you.'" [62]

"This is a unique event," said Nate. "Here we are at the house of someone who used to enforce Herod's tax laws, and he's throwing a party with all the tax cheaters invited."

"I heard that," said a man just coming in the gate. "I'm Issa, the most famous smuggler in Capernaum. I spent a lot of energy sneaking stuff past Levi the Taxman so I wouldn't have to pay import and export taxes."

Matt said, "Yea, that's my dad. So how'd you get to be the most famous?"

"By getting caught," he said. "Perez from Tiberias caught me red-handed with the goods. I had to pay a hefty fine to get myself out of prison. But now I'm baptized and legit, and making more money than I ever did smuggling. I'm so glad to be with the Jesus people now."

As Issa wandered off into the gathering crowd, John said, "I wonder if he's using any of that new money he's getting to help the orphans and widows?"

Nathanael said, "I doubt it. As a follower of Jesus, I expect he's still a work in progress."

Two men in raggedy clothing came in the gate. John recognized them as beggars that had been seen going from house to house asking for food. The first one asked, "Is this where the feast is being held?"

Matt said, "Yes it is. Who are you guys?"

"I'm Ishmael, and this is my friend Esau." [63]

Matt said, "Are you followers of Jesus?"

Esau said, "We are now! There's no place else to eat today in all of Capernaum."

John said, "Let them in, Matt. That's what Jesus would do."

As the two men joined the crowd, John said, "Do you think that's their real names?"

Nate said, "Not a chance. But before the day is over, they'll know who Jesus is."

28

TREASURE AND LIGHT

THURSDAY 9 SEPTEMBER AD 28, 10:00 AM

On the first day of the Jewish month of Elul, Jesus was teaching in the Capernaum synagogue again. He stood up and John gave him the scroll of Proverbs. Jesus unrolled the scroll and said, "Listen to what is written by Solomon, son of David!

> My people, if you receive my words
>   and treasure my commands within you,
> And make your ear attentive to wisdom
>   and incline your heart to understanding;
> Yes, if you call out for insight
>   and raise your voice for discernment;
> If you seek it like silver and search for it
>   as if it were hidden treasure,
> Then you will begin to understand
>   surrendering to the Lord
>   and find the precious knowledge of God." [64]

Jesus gave the scroll back to John and sat down. He said, "To what can we compare the kingdom of God? What parable shall we use for it?

"The kingdom of God is like treasure which a man finds hidden in a field. In jubilation he hides it again and sells all that he owns to buy that field.

"And again, the kingdom of God is like a merchant searching for a fine pearl. When he finds the pearl of great value, he sells everything he has just to buy it.[65]

"No one lights a lamp then covers it with a basket, or puts it under a bed or down in the cellar. A lamp is put on a stand so those who come in can see the light. But nothing is secret that won't become public, and nothing is hidden won't come to the light and be known.

"Your eye is the lamp of your body. If your eye is clear, your whole body is full of light. But if it is clouded over, you are full of darkness. So watch out that the light in you is not blotted out. If your body is full of light, with no darkness, it will be bright as a lamp on its lampstand."

Then he said, "If anyone has ears to hear, let him hear. Take care how you listen; for to the one who hears, more will be given, and from the one who does not hear, even what it seems he has heard will be taken away."[66]

With John beside him, Jesus was on his way back to Perpetua's house along with the Twelve and the Four. He said to them, "My children, the treasure you seek is not to be hidden but to be put on the lampstand. The wisdom you gain is to be shared and not kept secret. Have you understood all these things?"

They said, "Yes, teacher."

"Good. Every teacher of the Law who becomes a disciple of the kingdom of God is like a master of a house. Out of his treasure box he brings both new things and old things"[67]

29

Cost of Discipleship

THURSDAY 30 SEPTEMBER AD 28, 4:00 AM

The westerly hills behind Capernaum were becoming tinged with the first hint of light from the eastern sky. A few sprinkles of rain had come earlier and then cleared. John was on a hilltop with Jesus, who was praying about a stone's throw away. John ran out of things to pray for, and watched the approaching dawn as it overpowered the light of the fading stars.

Jesus got up and came over to John. He said, "My disciples need to wake up. They have become drowsy and lifeless; they're losing their saltiness. Today I will teach again by the sea. Go tell Simon Peter to have a boat or two ready for me offshore. Spread the word to the disciples that I'll be teaching at sunrise. And bring my scroll of Amos."

John knocked a second time on Matthew's gate, a bit louder this time. After a minute, Sarah opened it and said, "John! What's going on? I was just going to help get breakfast together for the disciples here. Would you like a bite?"

"That'd be good, thanks. Fix a bite for me to carry to Jesus, too. I was up in the hills praying with Jesus and then stopped at Perpetua's house to wake up the disciples. Jesus is gonna be teaching us at dawn by the lake, and I need to wake the disciples here. And I have to help bring boats over to the teaching spot."

"What's that you're carrying?"

"It's Jesus' scroll of the prophet Amos."

Sarah said, "I haven't seen one like that before. The one at the synagogue has all twelve of those prophets on a single scroll."

"Yeah, I know. Jesus has a big collection of scrolls. They're the inheritance he chose when his father Joseph died. And after that I think he got some others as well."

John handed the scroll to Jesus, who opened it and began reading:

> The one who placed the stars in the heavens
>   and brings morning from the deep
>   and darkens day into night;
> Who calls forth the waters of the sea
>   and pours them on the earth;
> Yahweh is his name.
> He it is who flashes ruin upon the mighty,
>   yes, destruction on them in their fortresses.[68]

"My friends, you have been blessed with a time of feasting. But do not become weak from feasting and fall asleep. For a time is coming when feasting will be taken away, when song and music will depart. Yet be strong. Let your justice roll down like waters upon the earth, and your uprightness like an ever flowing stream. [69]

"Only the Father knows the time of the end. But when it comes it will bring war, and famine, and death, and martyrs for our cause, and terror. There will be great trumpet calls, and hail, and fire, and blood, and mighty signs in the heavens. The evil one will be turned loose on the earth for his appointed time.[70]

"But before that time persecution will come upon you, and you will be brought before rulers and kings to be questioned. Some of you will be arrested and flogged, and some will be thrown into prison or be killed.

"The day of the political New Year comes upon us next week. Let the trumpet call of the New Year remind you that the Father holds your life in his hand, and that the Day of the Lord is coming with destruction.

"Do not think that I've come to bring peace to the earth. I have not come to bring peace, but a sword. For I have come to set a man against his father, a daughter against her mother, a daughter-in-law against her mother-in-law. Your enemies will come from your own household.

"The one who loves father or mother more than me isn't ready for me. The one who loves son or daughter more than me isn't ready for me. And the one who doesn't take up his cross to follow me isn't ready for me.

"Whoever finds his life will lose it, and whoever loses his life for my sake will find it. Whoever is not with me is against me, and whoever does not gather with me will be scattered."

Jesus continued with this theme, warning against the coming persecution and urging his disciples to remain strong in their faith.[71]

As the day went on Beon and Bohan, the Bashan brothers, arrived by foot from Capernaum and worked their way in close to the disciples. Then John's father Zebedee arrived in his fishing boat with his servants Samuel and Sheva, after dropping off two paying passengers from Bethsaida. They had sailed into Capernaum with the help of a gentle breeze from the east. Zebedee anchored next to Peter's fishing boat and Philip's rowboat, while Jesus continued schooling his disciples on the shore.

The sun slipped down behind the western hills, and Jesus was weary from teaching all day. But a great crowd of people had gathered behind the disciples around Jesus, and there was no way back to town except to deploy the stronger men to force open a corridor.

Jesus said, "Let's go across to the other side of the lake."

John was shocked. He had been looking forward to a nice supper at Perpetua's house and his comfy sleeping pallet upstairs.

The disciples began milling about as the boats were brought to shore. Tobias, a disciple from Capernaum, came to Jesus and said, "Lord, let me first go and bury my father."

Jesus looked on him kindly and said, "Leave the dead to bury their own dead, Tobias, and you follow me."

Then Gemariah, the young teacher of the Law, came up to Jesus and said, "Great Teacher, I will follow you wherever you go."

But Jesus grinned at him and said, "Foxes have holes, and birds of the air have nests, but the *Son of Man* has nowhere to lay his head."

So Jesus left the crowd and got into Peter's boat just as he was, and his disciples followed just as they were, without any preparations for travel. Other boats were also there, and some of those made ready to follow Jesus across the lake. [72]

John climbed into Peter's boat with Jesus and most of the Twelve, with also Concordia and Mary of Magdala. Thirteen in the boat was a crowd, but Jesus found space at the back to lay his head on a cushion and rest.

Big James went with Philip to help him with his rowboat. Beon and Bohan dithered on shore, but as the rowboat pushed off, they ran to jump into in with James and Philip. With four practiced oarsmen they would have enough power to run rings around the big fishing boats.

Zebedee and his servants were in his boat, and others began to climb in. There came Perez from Tiberias, Matthias from Cana, Joses from Ephraim, and Simon the Leper from Bethany. Matt Jr. climbed into Zebedee's boat and Gemariah followed him, leaving Tobias on the shore confused. As the boat began to pull away, Tobias dashed into the water and clambered into the boat, lifted up by Matt and Gemariah. That brought the total to twelve aboard Zebedee's boat.

They set out with Philip's rowboat in the lead, followed by the large vessels of Peter and Zebedee. Behind them were three more boats owned by spectators, with a few followers of Jesus on board who didn't make it into the first three boats. Big James set a course for just south of the city of Sussita, on the far side of the lake opposite Tiberias.

The wind was against them. These twenty-seven foot boats had flat bottoms so they could come in close to shore to catch fish. But since they had no keels, they were not well suited for using their sails to tack against the wind. So John took a first turn silently pulling at the oars against the increasing headwind, and thinking about what Jesus had been teaching today.

30

STORMS AND DEMONS

FRIDAY 1 OCTOBER AD 28, 2:00 AM

John and Thaddeus were using clay bowls to bail water. Peter, Andrew, Nathanael, and Simon of Hebron were pulling at the oars. Matthew was at the tiller position, using the steering oar.

The breeze against them had turned into a stiff wind with stinging rain. The spectator boats had long since given up and turned back. Zebedee's boat could be seen through the rain, but Philip's rowboat was nowhere in sight. John worried about his brother James and Philip.

A great swirling windstorm had just struck them, with waves breaking water into the boat. Thomas and Judas began bailing water using their hands. Mary the Magdalene was softly crying. The boat was being swamped, and they were filling with water and were in danger.

But Jesus was in the stern, still asleep on the cushion. In a flash of anger, Concordia went and woke Jesus, saying, "Master, Master, we're going to die! Don't you care?"

Jesus sat up and looked around. Then he stood up, stretched out his arms, and said to the wind and sea, "Peace! Be still!"

The wind stopped at once. The sea grew calm. The surface of the lake reflected the sky like a mirror. The rain stopped. Clouds parted. Stars could be seen.

John was stunned. Mary stopped crying and wiped her face. The rest of the disciples were amazed and silent.

Jesus said to them, "Why were you so afraid? Do you still have no faith?" Then he sat down on the cushion and comforted Mary.

The disciples were filled with great fear. Little James leaned over and said to John, "What kind of man is this? Even the wind and sea obey his commands!" [73]

Peter said, "Look, there's Sussita up on the hill!" The sky was beginning to light up, and the sun was hiding behind the small hilltop city.

"We only have to pull south a little more," said John, "and we'll be at the place my brother picked out. It's one of my dad's best fishing spots."

Thaddeus said, "Where are we, anyway?"

Simon the Zealot answered him. "The Romans who live in that town up there call it Hippos. We're in the district of Rome's Ten Towns. This territory is full of Gerasenes, Gadarenes, Ammonites, and all other sorts of Romans and Roman sympathizers. There's a few Jews, but I wouldn't feel safe living here."

Zebedee's boat was in the lead, and they were approaching the shore. John said, "Look, there's Philip's boat!"

"Yeah," said Thaddeus, "and look, way over there on the hillside. I see a big herd of pigs! There must be a couple thousand of them!"

Big James and the three with him met them on the beach, and they helped bring the two big boats to shore. Then as Jesus stepped out onto the sand, a voice was heard crying out loudly,

"Jesus of Nazareth, we know you! You are the Son of God!" Two men were running down the hillside to meet them. One of them was not wearing any clothes, and his body was covered with bruises and bloody cuts.

Jesus called out, "Come out of those men, you foul spirits!"

Immediately one of the men stopped and sat down, perplexed. But the one with no clothes ran up to the shoreline. He fell down in front of Jesus and cried out again, "What have you to do with us, Jesus, Son of the Most High God? Are you here to torment us before our time? I beg you, don't torture us."

Jesus said to him sternly, "Tell me your name, spirit!"

The man replied, "Our name is Legion, for we are many. I beg of you; don't send us into the abyss! If you cast us out, send us into that herd of pigs. Let us go in to them!"

Jesus said, "Be it as you have said. Begone, Legion!" And as the foul spirits came out of the man, the herd of pigs rushed down the bank into the sea and drowned in the water. The herdsmen on the hillside saw what was happening, and ran away into the city.

Zebedee said, "I'm going fishing."

"I'm going with you," said Big James.

"Me too!" said John. He helped Samuel and Sheva launch the boat.

This was like old times. It had been fifteen months since John had gone fishing with his family. They used the throw nets, and each time they cast a net out into the lake they brought in two or three fish.

When they had three dozen fish, they brought the boat in to shore. Simon the Zealot and Judas of Kerioth had gathered wood and built a fire. Jesus began roasting the fish over the fire and passing them out as they were ready. None of the disciples had eaten since yesterday morning, and they were ravenous.

The man who had suffered from the legion of demons was fully clothed now. He and his friend were sitting at Jesus' feet. Both of them were now in their right minds, eating fire-roasted fish.

Four men in Jewish clothing were coming down the hill from the city, two of them carrying sacks. When they arrived they saw the two men that had been plagued by demons sitting at Jesus' feet. Many of the disciples were sleeping on the beach, exhausted from the battle with the overnight storm.

John and Andrew rose to meet the visitors, who asked, "Are you disciples of Jesus of Nazareth?"

John said, "Yes. How did you know?"

"The herdsmen for the pigs came into town this morning with a wild tale about our local demoniac confronting some boatmen and then chasing all their pigs into the sea. We suspected that something powerful had happened and we thought it might be the new prophet Jesus we have been hearing about."

Jesus spoke from beside the fire. "I am Jesus of Nazareth. Would you like a bite of fire-roasted fish? I have four left over from our morning meal."

The man replied, "Thank you very much, but we have already eaten. Welcome to our district, Great Teacher. I am Josiah, son of Joram. We are honored to meet you, but I fear the Romans in town will not welcome you."

Jesus said, "I am sent only to the children of Abraham. The time for Romans to hear the good news of the kingdom of God has not yet been fulfilled."

Peter and Big James and Philip and Nathanael gathered around the four visitors and told them the correct tale of what happened when they arrived, including the demons that had gone into the herd of pigs.

Josiah said, "This man who had the legion of demons was very dangerous. He's been living in the wilderness, and was so fierce that no one dared to pass through here. Night and day he would cry out among the tombs and cut himself with stones.

"For a long time he has worn no clothes, and the men of the city tried to arrest and confine him. But no one could bind him safely, not even with a chain. They would bind him with shackles and chains, but he wrenched the chains apart and broke the shackles in pieces.

"The demons drove him into the tombs, and no one had the strength to subdue him. The second man we know little about. He's been seen here only recently." [74]

Nathanael asked, "What is your situation here? I didn't know there were Jews in Sussita."

"There are just 25 of us, with barely enough men to form a prayer group. We're merchants who deal in import and export of goods, and exchanges with the caravan trade. The people of the city pledge their allegiance to Rome, and they only tolerate us. If war broke out between Rome and the Jews, there are some hotheads who would like to kill us immediately."

The men gave two sacks to Peter, and Josiah said, "Here, we have brought some bread for you. We owe thanks to Jesus for ridding our coastland of a dangerous menace." The four men thanked Jesus and the disciples, and said they would return after the Sabbath with more food.

Jesus said, "Thank you for the bread. You will not lose your blessing."

Jesus was taking a nap under a tree near the shore. The other men had begun to wake up and move around. Beon and Bohan came over to where John and Andrew were sitting with Nathanael and Matt.

Nate said, "Well, Bashan boys, I guess we're going to have to call you disciples of Jesus now."

Beon said, "I suppose so. It looked to us like Jesus needed a security detail. So we decided to hide our short swords under our clothes and make sure no one messes with him."

Andrew said, "Big James and my brother think the same thing. They're carrying short swords to protect Jesus from assassins."

With a twinkle in his eye Nate said, "You guys are a long way from your nets and fishing lines. I thought you weren't going to give them up until you saw the Messiah sitting on his throne in Jerusalem."

Bohan said, "Oh, we still have them put away in Capernaum. If this Jesus thing doesn't work out, we can always go back to fishing."

Tobias and Gemariah came over to where the men were talking and sat down. Matt said, "Tobias, you almost missed the boat when we left! What happened?"

"I asked Jesus if I could stay behind to take care of my father's affairs," said Tobias. "But Jesus told me to follow him. I was having trouble deciding what to do."

"I don't understand," said Matt. "What was the problem?"

"My father is getting old, and may pass away in the next few years. If I leave him and he dies, my uncle next door will take care of burying him and settling his affairs. But then I will lose my place in the family, and my uncle will get my inheritance."

John said, "Is there a lot to take care of?"

"Not really—mainly our house in Capernaum. I had to decide what was more important, my place in the family or my place with Jesus. I'm glad I chose Jesus."

"Good choice," said Gemariah. "I had to make the same choice too. I came to that insight over the last few months of hearing Jesus teach."

Matt said, "What about your plan to start a school for teachers of the Law?"

Gemariah said, "That has all changed. I was a disciple of Nicodemus. He's a good man, skilled in the Law, and very wise. When I turned thirty, I was going to start a school to teach Scripture and the wisdom of Nicodemus."

Matt said, "So what are you gonna do now?"

"I decided if I ever start a school, I'm going to teach nothing but Jesus and his message of the kingdom. What's happening here is far greater than Nicodemus."

31

Personae Non Gratae

WEDNESDAY 6 OCTOBER AD 28, 4:00 PM

On Saturday many of the people from Sussita had come to see what happened, and to see the wild man who had the demons. Instead, they saw the formerly wild man sitting at the feet of Jesus, clothed and in his right mind, and this struck them with awe and fear.

More had come to gawk on Sunday from the nearby villages. The legend of the wild man spread through the Ten Towns, and throughout the week people arrived from Gadara and Philoteria nearby, from Abila and Capitolias to the east, and even from Gerasa and Ammon far to the south.

Many of them were afraid to approach Jesus, thinking he might harm them with a bolt from heaven or some other mighty sign. The people of the surrounding countryside began to beg Jesus to leave the area, for they were seized with fear.

On Wednesday afternoon a delegation of men in official Roman garb came down the hill from Sussita. Peter, Andrew, and John went out to meet them while Big James and Simon the Zealot kept a wary eye on them.

Peter said, "What do you seek?"

The man leading the group replied in Greek, "Greetings. I am Lord Mayor of the Sovereign Roman *polis* of Hippos. We have been in conference with several of the Ten Towns, and we have come to a decision on what to do about the disturbance your people caused this Friday. We are officially notifying you that your group has been declared *Personae non Gratae*."

Peter said, "Pardon me, but I don't speak Latin. What does '*Personae non Gratae*' mean?"

The mayor looked at Peter with contempt. "*Personae non Gratae* means that you and your group have officially been declared unwelcome. You must leave our territory, for we cannot guarantee your safety if you should remain here."

"Very well," said Peter. "We will depart in the morning, as we had already planned. Thank you for your notification."

Most of the Jews from Sussita came down in the morning to thank them and see them off. They brought gifts of food and clothing for the two men who had been freed from foul spirits.

As Jesus was getting into the boat, both of the men begged Jesus to be allowed to stay with him. Jesus said, "No, but go home to your friends and family and tell everyone how much God has done for you, and how he has had mercy on you." Jesus got into Peter's boat, and all three boats cast off to return to Capernaum.

Later, John learned that the two men travelled through all the Ten Towns to proclaim how much Jesus had done for them.[75]

32

Twelve Years

THURSDAY 7 OCTOBER AD 28, 12:00 NOON

When Jesus arrived on the shore near Capernaum, a large crowd welcomed him. They were all waiting for him to say something, wondering what changes the New Year might bring.

Jesus stepped onto the shore and said, "Today is the Feast of Trumpets, the beginning of a new year for the reigns of kings. A new year heralds a new beginning, so examine yourselves. Look back on your mistakes of the past year, and repent. Today if you are willing, you can begin a new life. Repent and make yourselves ready for the kingdom of God."

Jesus stayed on the shore for an hour, teaching repentance and the kingdom of God. Then as he and his disciples began to walk into Capernaum, the crowd pressed in around him, swarming and shifting. John struggled to stay near Jesus in the crowd.

One woman came up behind Jesus and touched the fringe of his garment. Jesus immediately turned about in the mass of people and said, "Who touched my clothing?"

All the people around him denied it. Peter said, "Master, the crowd is surrounding you and pressing in on you!"

But Jesus said, "Someone touched me, for I felt power go out from me." And he looked around to see who had done it. When the woman saw that she couldn't hide from his gaze, she came trembling in fear. She fell down before Jesus and told him the whole truth.

In the presence of the entire crowd she said, "Master, I've had a discharge of blood for twelve years now. I suffered greatly under many doctors, and spent all my money on them. But I didn't get any better; instead, I grew worse.

"I heard the reports about you and thought that if I touched even the fringe of your garment I would be made well. That's why I touched you, and instantly I was healed. The flow of blood dried up, and I felt in my body that I was healed of my disease."

Jesus told her, "Take heart, daughter. Your faith has made you well. Rejoice in your healing."

And he said, "Go in peace. Your twelve years of misery and sickness are over. Today is a new year and a new beginning. Today you can begin a new life. So seek God and his kingdom, and even more blessings will be added to you." [76]

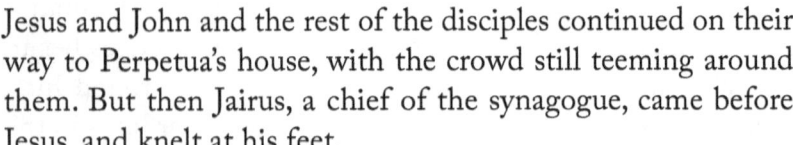

Jesus and John and the rest of the disciples continued on their way to Perpetua's house, with the crowd still teeming around them. But then Jairus, a chief of the synagogue, came before Jesus, and knelt at his feet.

Jairus begged Jesus earnestly, saying, "My little daughter, my only child, is sick and dying! She's been weak and sickly all of her twelve years. But come and lay your hands on her, and she will be made well and live."

Jesus went with him, and the crowd followed, thronging around him. As they passed by the synagogue, someone from Jairus' house came and said to him, "Your daughter has died. Why trouble the teacher any further?"

But Jesus overheard this, and said to Jairus, "Do not fear, only believe, and your daughter will be in good health."

When they arrived at Jairus' house there were flute players and professional mourners outside wailing and making a commotion. Jesus said, "Go away, all of you, for the girl is not dead but sleeping." But they scoffed at him.

Then when he entered the house, the people inside were in turmoil, weeping and wailing. Jesus said to them, "Why are you making an uproar and weeping? The child has not died; she is just sleeping."

But they laughed at him, saying "She's already dead!" So Jesus put them all outside. He allowed no one inside with him except Peter, John, and James, and the parents of the girl.

They went in to where the child was, and taking her by the hand Jesus said, "Little girl, I say to you, rise up." She got up at once and began walking! Her parents were overcome with wonder.

John became weepy-eyed as he watched Jairus and his wife and daughter embrace one another and hold on to each other.

Jesus said, "Your daughter's twelve years of weakness and sickness are over. Today is a new year and a new beginning. Today she begins a new life, as you can also. So seek the kingdom of God, and even more blessing will be added to you."

Jesus strictly charged them that no one should know about this, and told them to give the child something to eat. But the report of what happened went through all Capernaum and all the towns around the Sea of Galilee.[77]

33

You Can't Go Home

FRIDAY 5 NOVEMBER AD 28, 4:00 PM

Here they were in Nazareth again, getting ready to attend synagogue. But the synagogue doors were shut, and no one from town was here yet for the Sabbath evening service. Jesus was beginning another tour of the villages of Galilee, taking twenty-seven of his disciples with him. They were resting after a vigorous journey from Capernaum.

John said, "Does it feel good to be home again, Teacher?"

Jesus said, "I was a child in this town, John. I look at the places I went to then, and the things I did then, and they are far away from me now, for I'm no longer a child. I was small then, but now I'm taller. I had the wisdom of happiness then, but now I have the wisdom that includes sadness. I remember childhood times here, but I can't go back to those times."

John said, "I felt like that this fall when I visited my parents for a week. Then when we went fishing at Sussita, it felt good at first. But I was sad when it was over, because I'm not a fisherman, I'm a disciple. But then I was glad I'm a disciple. It's confusing."

"Yes, John, that's what growing up is like. I grew up to be a construction worker, and although I lived here in Nazareth, I travelled around with my brothers to wherever the construction jobs were. It was rewarding, making buildings go up, or watching improvements being made, and knowing I had a part in it. But now that's behind me. Instead of building houses, I'm building the kingdom of God. Instead of being one of the workers, I'm the master builder."

"Doesn't it feel good to be the one in charge?"

"Believe me, John, sometimes I'd like to be one of the workers. But my Father in heaven has sent me to be in charge, and I have a calling to fulfill."

John said, "Hey, there's Nathanael and Matthias, coming up the hill." Nate and his cousin had been sent two days ahead to arrange lodging in Nazareth.

Jesus said, "Go get Peter and Matthew and James of Alpheus and we'll have a conference."

Peter said, "Okay, Nate, let's hear your report."

Nathanael said, "We didn't get much of a welcome here. We found some houses where we could stay, but the master of the house would be doing it out of duty, not because he wanted to. So we'll be staying with the brothers of Jesus. James the Just can take ten of us, while Simon and Jude will take six each.

"Joseph already has guests, 'cause Jesus' two sisters from Sepphoris are here visiting. But his house is larger, so he can take six of us also. It's not roomy, but it'll work. And Jesus has been invited to speak at synagogue tomorrow morning."

Jesus said, "There are three sleeping rooms at James' house. The four women will take the girls' room, Michael and Thomas will sleep in the parents' room with my brother James, and Philip and the Zebedees will sleep in the boys' room with me.

Peter, take five disciples to stay with you at Joseph's house. Matthew, take five for Simon's house. James my Levite, take the last five to stay at Jude's. And be of good cheer, for we rest well tonight."

34

Hometown Humbling

SATURDAY 6 NOVEMBER AD 28, 10:00 AM

It was Sabbath morning, and the first day of the month of Cheshvan. Jesus stood up in the synagogue of Nazareth, and John presented him with the scroll of Isaiah. He unrolled it and began to read:

> On this mountain, the Lord of heaven's armies
>> will make for all peoples a feast of rich
>> food, a banquet of well-aged wine,
>> of rich food full of marrow,
>> of aged wine well refined.
>
> On this mountain, he will swallow up
>> the darkness that is cast over all peoples,
>> the veil that is spread over all nations.
>
> He will swallow up death forever;
>> the Lord God will wipe away tears
>> from all faces;
>> he will remove the reproach of his people
>> from all the earth, for the Lord has spoken.

It will be said on that day,
> "Behold, this is our God;
> we have waited for him,
> that he might save us.
> This is the Lord; we have waited for him;
> let us be glad and rejoice in his salvation. [78]

Jesus rolled up the scroll, gave it to John, and sat down. The whole room was quiet as they waited for him to speak.

He said, "Who shall be invited to the great banquet of God our Father? Who will enter God's kingdom where death lives no more? What is his kingdom like? To what can we compare the kingdom of God?

"The kingdom of God may be compared to a king who gave a wedding feast for his son, and sent his servants to call those who were invited to the wedding feast. But they would not come. So he sent more servants, saying, 'Tell those who are invited, "See, I have prepared my banquet. My oxen and my fattened calves have been slaughtered, and everything is ready. Come to the wedding feast."' But they paid no attention and went off, one to his farm, and another to his business.

"And others seized his servants, and treated them shamefully, and killed them. The king was furious, and he sent troops to destroy those murderers and burn their city.

"Then he said to his servants, 'The wedding feast is ready, but those invited were not worthy. Go then to the main roads and invite as many as you find to the wedding feast.' And those servants went out into the roads and gathered all whom they found, both bad and good. So the wedding hall was filled with guests.

"But when the king came in to look at the guests, he saw there a man who had no wedding garment. And he said to him, 'Friend, how did you get in here without a wedding garment?'

"But the man had no answer. So the king said to the attendants, 'Bind him hand and foot and cast him into the outer darkness, where there will be weeping and gnashing of teeth.'[79]

"Many will be invited, but few will be chosen. Have you answered your invitation? Do you have your wedding garment? Have you repented of your sin? Even today, you may choose."

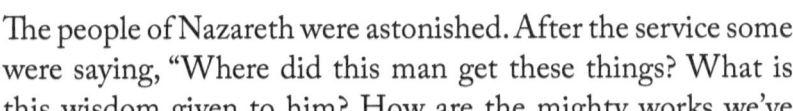

The people of Nazareth were astonished. After the service some were saying, "Where did this man get these things? What is this wisdom given to him? How are the mighty works we've heard about done by his hands?"

Others said, "Isn't this the carpenter's son? Isn't his mother called Mary? And aren't his brothers James and Joseph and Simon and Jude? Aren't his sisters here with us? Where then did this man get these things?" And they took offense at him.

Two men came up to Jesus and said, "How can you teach these things? We know you, and we know that you have not been trained by the teachers of the Law!"

Jesus said to them, "A prophet is not without honor, except in his hometown and among his own household."

And Jesus couldn't do many works of power in Nazareth, except to lay his hands on a few sick people after the service and heal them. Their unbelief was astonishing.[80]

Jesus took John and some of his disciples on a tour of the countryside around Nazareth, and visited the thirty acre field that his brothers Simon and Jude farmed. At sunset they returned to their lodgings.

John said, "Teacher, why did these people reject you at the synagogue? I thought they were your friends."

Jesus said, "A darkness has been cast over them. A veil is covering their eyes, and their ears are stopped up with their own beliefs and perceptions. Pray for them, that they might see the light and turn to their Father in heaven."

Concordia came from the kitchen. "Dinner's ready. Either James the Just is a very good cook or he had some helpers sneak in here to prepare a feast for us."

"Ah, wonderful," said Jesus. "And yes, my brother knows how to cook."

35

PARTING OF THE WAYS

SUNDAY 5 DECEMBER AD 28, 12:00 NOON

Jesus and his disciples stepped out of the synagogue of Shiqmona and into the street. He had healed and taught here much of yesterday, but the people begged him to come back for a second day of teaching today, on this first day of the Jewish month of Kislev.

A fresh breeze was blowing onshore from the Great Sea. Small fishing boats and grand sailing vessels were plying the coastline for trade, travel, and trawling. Just inland was the sacred peak of Mount Carmel, once visited by the ancient prophets Elijah and Elisha.

Jesus called to his disciples, "Walk with me for a ways, for we have come to a parting of our companies."

John was startled. He thought, "*What! What can Jesus mean?*"

Nate and Philip and some of the other disciples had gone to see the docks at seaside, but most of the rest were walking with Jesus, who led them east toward Mount Carmel.

Jesus said, "Friends, we've gone through the cities and villages of southern Galilee, teaching in synagogues, homes, and on the streets. We've proclaimed the good news of the kingdom and healed diseases and afflictions.

"I have seen the crowds, and they cry out for compassion. They are harassed and helpless, like sheep without a shepherd. To the north, the rest of Galilee cries out for good news. To the south, all of Judea cries out for good news. Which way shall we go? The harvest is plentiful, but the laborers are few. Pray to the Lord to send laborers out into his harvest. [81]

"I have elected twelve of you to be my emissaries—my representatives—to be sent on missions in my name both near and far, and to proclaim the good news of the kingdom. Now it's time for you to go out. The Twelve will go south to the cities and villages of Judea, and I will go with the others to northern Galilee."

Matt said, "What time are we leaving?"

Jesus laughed. "Ah, eager to go, are you? No, we're not leaving today. Peter, gather the Twelve in the upper room where we stayed, and I'll bring final instructions to you, two hours from now. Perez, tell the other disciples I'll meet them tomorrow morning in the upper room where you stayed. Now all of you leave me, while I have a few more words with this eager disciple."

John watched as Jesus and Matt walked up the path leading to Mount Carmel. He thought about his own walk with the Master, on the beach at Capernaum more than a year ago.

Jesus sat down in the upper room with the Twelve gathered around him. He said, "My friends, it's time for you to be sent out. But I am not sending you alone; you will go out two by two. Peter, go with James son of Zebedee. Andrew, go with John. Philip, go with Nathanael. Thomas, go with Matthew. James my Levite, go with your son Judas Thaddeus. And Simon my Zealot, go with Judas my man from Kerioth. Stay together, and strengthen one another.

"I give you authority over foul spirits; do not fear them. Cast them out in my name when you find them and banish them to the wilderness. In my name you have authority to heal every disease and every affliction you find. Heal the sick, raise the dead, and cleanse the lepers.[82]

"Don't go among those who are strangers to God and the words of Moses. Don't enter any town of Samaritans. Go instead to the lost sheep of the house of Israel. As you go, proclaim aloud, 'The kingdom of God is at hand!'

"Don't take anything for your journey except sandals and a walking stick. Don't take spare sandals, or an extra tunic, or a shepherd's club. Simon Peter and James son of Zebedee, give up your swords—yes, I know you have them.

"You received the word without paying; give it back without being paid. Don't carry gold or silver or copper in your belts, or a pack for your journey, for the worker deserves his meals.

"When you enter a town or village, find out who is worthy in it and stay there until you leave. When you go into a house, greet it. If the house is worthy, let your peace come upon it. But if it is not worthy, let your peace return to you.

"But if a town will not receive you or will not listen to your words, shake off the dust from your feet as a testimony against them when you leave. Truly I say to you, it will be more bearable on judgment day for the land of Sodom and Gomorrah than for that town."[83]

And Jesus said, "Have you understood all this? Have you any questions?"

Everyone said they understood. Then Peter said, "What are we to do with our swords?"

"The other disciples can carry them to Capernaum. There will come a day when you may need them, for you will be counted as criminals because of me. People will think they are acting righteously if they kill you."

And Jesus said, "Listen! I'm sending you out as sheep into a pack of wolves, so be wise as serpents and innocent as doves. Beware of men, for they'll deliver you to courts and flog you in synagogues. They'll drag you before governors and kings for my sake, to bear witness before the world of your testimony. When this happens, don't be anxious over how to speak or what to say. What you are to say will be given to you in that hour. It won't be you speaking, but the Spirit of your Father speaking through you. [84]

"Are you not my disciples? But a disciple isn't above his teacher, or a servant above his master. It's enough for the disciple to be like his teacher, and the servant like his master. So if they've called the master of the house Beelzebub, just think how they will slander those of his household!

"What I told you in the dark, say in the light. What you heard whispered, proclaim on the housetops. Don't be afraid of those who kill the body but can't kill the soul. Rather fear the one who can throw body and soul into the place of eternal punishment.

"Aren't two sparrows sold for a tenth of a denarius? Yet not one of them will fall to the ground without your Father's knowledge. But you, even the hairs of your head are numbered. So don't be afraid. You're worth more than many sparrows.[85]

"Everyone who accepts me before men, I will accept before my Father in heaven. But whoever denies me before men, I will deny before my Father in heaven. Likewise, whoever receives you receives me, and whoever receives me receives the one who sent me.

The one who receives a prophet because he is a prophet will receive a prophet's reward. And whoever gives one of my little ones even a cup of cold water because he's my disciple, truly I say to you, he will in no way lose his reward." [86]

———•••●•••———

John climbed the stairs into the upper room, followed by Concordia, Perez, and Gemariah. Waiting for them were Peter, Matthew, Nathanael, Little James, and Judas of Kerioth. Peter greeted them and said, "Thanks for coming, guys, and thanks, John for going to get them. We're leaving tomorrow, and we wanted to take care of a couple things."

"Thanks," said Perez. "We've been wondering about a few things ourselves, but I suppose Jesus will clear things up in the morning."

Peter said, "Yes Perez, it looks like Jesus is going to use you to round up the disciples when he wants them. Welcome to the club."

"Thanks. But if he wants to call back the disciples that he released to their homes, I don't know who or where they all are."

Peter said, "I'm not sure I can remember all of them myself. But you can use Joseph *bar* Sabbas for that. He has the complete roll call. Also, Beon and Bohan both have short swords to protect Jesus from assassins; they should stay near him when he's in a crowd."

Matthew said, "Gemariah, I've been the acting scribe for the disciples, and I've also been writing down the memorable things that Jesus says or does. I have parchment and ink for you so you can take over from me if you wish."

"Thanks, Matthew, that would be an honor," said Gemariah.

Nathanael said, "Perez, you can use my cousin Matthias as an advance scout; he's good at arranging lodging. He and I have also been perimeter lookouts when we have big crowds.

And if you need anyone to translate for Greek speakers, Simon the Leper is good at that, and can fill in for Philip."

"Thanks for that, Nate," said Perez.

Little James said, "Perez, you can use my brother Joses as a Jerusalem contact. He's good at finding out what the high priests and Pharisees are doing there."

Judas of Kerioth stepped forward and gave Concordia the money bag. He said, "Concordia, we've been talking, and we think you should carry the purse for your group, unless Jesus has another idea. You can use Mary Magdalene to help you shop for food."

Concordia said, "Oh my goodness. Okay, I can handle that. But I'm not sure I can handle being separated from my husband for two months."

Simon Peter took her into his arms and said, "I'm feeling the same, my love."

John said, "And I'm gonna miss being around Jesus twenty-four seven. It looks like Jesus picked Matt Junior to take my place while I'm gone. I'm gonna go talk with Matt for a while."

36

Six Roads

MONDAY 6 DECEMBER AD 28, 8:00 AM

The Twelve finished their morning meal, which their Shiqmona hosts had brought up to them an hour after dawn. Andrew said, "John, did you go out and pray with Jesus this morning?"

John said, "No. I woke up an hour before sunrise and Jesus was already gone. All his stuff was gone also. I went over to the other house at dawn, but Jesus was upstairs teaching and the door was shut. So I came back here."

Philip said, "I guess there's nothing for us to do but hit the road, then."

John said, "Where you gonna go, Philip?"

"Nate and I want to check out the towns of Antipatris and Ha-Ramathaim.[87] What about you, Thomas?

"Matthew and I are going to Joppa and Jamnia. Joppa's a big city and I think Jamnia's a little smaller. Tad, where are you going?"

"My dad and I are going to Gophna and Anathoth. Anathoth is an ancient Levite town where the prophet Jeremiah was born. What about you, Peter?"

"Big James and I are going to Lydda and Gazara. Lydda's a big town and Gazara's an old fortress. What about you, Andrew?"

"John and I are going to Emmaus and then Bethlehem. Jesus was born in Bethlehem, but I don't think he has any disciples there yet. How about you, Simon?"

"Judas and I are going south and inland to the village of Bayt Letepha. There's a lot of anti-Roman sentiment in that region, and we want them to hear about Jesus and the kingdom of God. And after that we're aiming for the city of Judah."

Nate said, "Tad, you're going to be right there where you can attend the Festival of Lights in Jerusalem a month from now." [88]

"Hey, I wanna go to the Festival," said John.

Matthew said, "Why don't we plan to all meet for the festival? We could visit and then go on from there to take the news of the kingdom to more villages."

"Sounds like a good idea to me," said Peter. "We can check on how we're all doing and what we might be able to do better."

James the Levite said, "We can all make these grand plans, but if God isn't with us, nothing will happen. We need to pray every day, and sing to the Lord as we travel. Let's sing a psalm right now before we leave."

Tad picked a psalm, and the Twelve joined in to sing:

The Lord is my shepherd; I shall not be in want.
He makes me lie down in green pastures;
He leads me beside still waters.
He restores my soul;
He leads me in the right paths
    for his name's sake.
Though I walk the valley
    of the shadow of death,
I will fear no evil, for you are with me;

Your rod and your staff comfort me.
You spread a table for me among my enemies;
You anoint my head with oil,
    and my cup runs over.
Your goodness and mercy
    will follow me all my days, and
I will dwell in the house of the Lord forever. [89]

James the Levite led them in praying for safety, success, and inspiration for their work. Then the Twelve picked up their walking sticks and left the building, walking south on Via Maris, the great seacoast highway.

John felt really strange to be traveling without his pack, and without Jesus nearby. But then he started humming the psalm again and it made him feel better as they marched along.

37

Emmaus

Thursday 9 December AD 28, 1:00 pm

John and Andrew watched Simon and Judas walk away down a southbound dirt track, looking for the strange town of Bayt Letepha. Now there were just the two of them left.

Leaving Shiqmona, the Twelve had walked south to the major seaport of Caesarea, then on the next day to Antipatris. The following day they left Philip and Nathanael behind in Antipatris.

From there Little James and Thaddeus went eastbound to pass through Ha-Ramathaim on their way to Gophna. The remaining eight went south towards Lydda, but Matthew and Thomas turned west at an intersection that led to Joppa on the coast. Today, Peter and James had stayed behind in Lydda while the final four walked southeast to Emmaus.

Simon and Judas disappeared around a corner of the trail. Now it was just John and Andrew, alone in Emmaus. John was apprehensive. He said, "So what do we do, just knock on doors until we find someone who'll feed us?"

"Don't be so worried, John. We haven't missed a meal yet on this trip," said Andrew.

"Sorry," John said. "You're right."

"Let's walk back to the middle of town and see what's going on."

The middle of town was bisected by the stone-paved Roman highway that connected Lydda to Jerusalem. They began walking southeast, greeting a few people on the road. Then came a voice from behind them.

"John! What a surprise to see you here!"

They turned to see a youth about John's age. John said, "Elnathan! Good to see you! Andrew, this is Elnathan, a disciple of Nicodemus. Elnathan, this is my friend Andrew son of Jonas, a disciple of Jesus like me."

"Pleased to meet you," said Elnathan. "What brings you to Emmaus?"

Andrew said, "We have come to proclaim that the kingdom of God is at hand! John the Baptist was the first to announce it, but one who is mightier than he has come who brings the kingdom of God among us. That one is Jesus of Nazareth, son of David. If anyone wants peace with God, they need to repent and be baptized, and believe that Jesus is Lord."

Elnathan said, "Are you saying that Jesus is the Messiah?"

John said, "We'll let you decide that. But so far, all that Jesus has said and done matches what is written about the Messiah in the Law and the Prophets and the Writings. Andrew and I are witnesses to all these things."

Elnathan said, "We already had a man come to claim he was the Messiah, one Simon of Perea. He came thirty-two years ago and burned down Herod's palaces. All we got out of that was the Roman army, which came and burned down the whole city of Emmaus. We used to be an important city, but now we're hardly more than a village. The people who survived have returned, because here is where their fathers are buried."

"You'll find that Jesus is a gentle man," said Andrew. He teaches us to be good to our enemies, and to love those who hate us."

"I'd like to hear more about this," said Elnathan. "Where will you be staying tonight?"

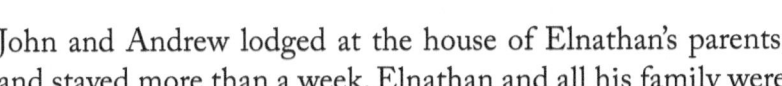

John and Andrew lodged at the house of Elnathan's parents, and stayed more than a week. Elnathan and all his family were baptized in the name of Jesus, along with a dozen of his friends from town.

Many more in Emmaus were also interested in Jesus and the coming of the kingdom. But they told the story of when two thousand Jews were crucified by the Romans because of the rebellion of Simon of Perea. All they could do then in response was to stop buying Roman pottery.

As John and Andrew prepared to depart, John said to Elnathan, "What will you do now? Are you still going to be a disciple of Nicodemus?"

"Well, I've finished my visit with my parents. I'm going to return to Nicodemus and ask permission to become a disciple of Jesus. If he refuses, I may leave him anyway. New things are happening that are more powerful than Nicodemus, even if he is a member of the Supreme Council."

"I'm looking forward to seeing you again, Elnathan."

"Yes, and I look forward to that too."

38

Twelve Tales

WEDNESDAY 5 JANUARY AD 29, 4:00 PM

John and Andrew were in the inner court around the Jerusalem temple, and were looking for the rest of the Twelve among the crowd for the Festival of Lights. The only ones missing now were Nathanael, Philip, Simon, and Judas. James the Levite and Thaddeus were already inside the temple.

Andrew said, "Well, let's go inside while there's still room. They'll be lighting the first candle of the Hanukkah lamp in less than an hour."

John said, "We must have missed the other guys. Maybe they're already inside. I was hoping to tell everyone we found a place to stay."

The six disciples filed into the temple, and immediately ran into Nate and Philip. Nate said, "I was just going out to tell you to come on in. Everybody's here but Simon and Judas."

John said, "I found a place for us to stay with some friends of Jesus. It's at the house of Mary and Martha and their brother Lazarus in Bethany. We can stay there for the whole eight days of the festival."

"Yeah, Tad told me," said Nate. "I'm looking forward to this. It's good to remember the rededication of the temple, and the miracle of one day's worth of oil lasting for eight days."

A company of Levites was singing a psalm, and the priests assigned for the reading of the special festival prayers were arriving to take their places. John found Tad in the crowd, and began singing with him. Simon and Judas arrived late, standing at the back of the crowd.

The Twelve were eating in a downstairs room with the family of Lazarus. John brought Martha and Mary up to date with what Jesus had been doing since they saw him last.

Peter said, "Well, that brings us up to last month. Now let's hear from each of us about what we've been doing since we left Jesus."

Nathanael said, "Philip and I stopped at Antipatris, surrounded by vineyards. The next morning, I started walking the streets of the city yelling, 'The kingdom of God is at hand! The kingdom of God is at hand!' I felt ridiculous. But finally a group of men stopped me and asked what in the world I was yelling about, and they listened to the message of Jesus. Philip and I baptized a dozen people in that city."

Philip said, "Then we went to Ha-Ramathaim. The farmers there insist the town is named after the tall women who founded it, which I thought was strange. But we met a rich man there who was intensely interested in Jesus and his message. He's a Pharisee landowner who's well-loved by the farmers who work for him.

"Nate and I spent three weeks teaching and discipling the rich man and his entire household. But he asked us to keep our work secret because of his connections with the Supreme Council, and begged us not to reveal his name as a disciple of Jesus. I told him Jesus said, 'Nothing is secret that won't become public,' but he just said, 'Let God's will be done.'"

James the Levite said, "Thaddeus and I went to Gophna, which the Romans use as a regional capitol. When we were approaching town, two lepers were standing near the road warning us not to come close to them. They were shouting 'Unclean! Unclean!' I told them about Jesus and asked them if they wanted to be cleansed of their skin disease."

Judas said, "Did you touch them?"

"Yes, I laid hands on them in the name of Jesus, and suddenly their skin became clear and healthy. I told them to go show themselves to a priest who would declare them clean. I told them their cleansing was a sign of the kingdom of God coming among us. We stayed in Gophna many days sharing the good news of the kingdom."

Thaddeus said, "We went on from there to Anathoth, and were doing the same thing. Then I saw a baby held by her mother who was very sick, burning up with fever. I laid hands on her and healed her in the name of Jesus. The people of Anathoth were amazed, and begged us to stay on with them to tell them more about Jesus. They want us to come back after the festival."

Matthew said, "Thomas and I went to Joppa and attended synagogue. A blind woman there was being led around by her husband. I anointed her eyes with oil and laid hands on her to pray for her sight. She immediately was able to see! We baptized many in the name of Jesus there."

Thomas said, "When Matthew and I were coming in to Jamnia, an old man came out of a pottery shop and yelled at us. He shouted, 'I know who you are! You're disciples of the Son of God! What do you want with us?' In the name of Jesus I commanded the foul spirit to come out of the man, and he was set free instantly! Some people from town saw it happen, and talked about it all through the city. Matthew and I baptized more than a dozen in that place."

Peter said, "Big James and I went to Lydda and proclaimed the good news for three days. Then when we went to synagogue I noticed a man who was a cripple, who couldn't walk without help. I anointed him and prayed for his healing, and right away his legs were strengthened and he could walk with no help. The whole synagogue was amazed, and started taking an interest in this 'good news' we were proclaiming. We baptized a few people, including the one who was a cripple."

Big James said, "Then we went to Gazara. The old fortress captured by our hero Simon Maccabeus is falling down and useless, but the palace Simon built for himself still stands. The Romans are using it as a government center. But Peter and I ignored all that and started proclaiming the kingdom of God and the name of Jesus, and we gained a few believers.

"Then one family came to me and asked if I would bless their three month old baby boy, who was sick. By the time I got to their house, the baby had died, and they had already called for the professional mourners. I went into the baby's room just like Jesus did and laid hands on her. Immediately she woke up and was hungry. Then many more people in town believed in Jesus and came to be baptized."

John said, "When Andrew and I got to Emmaus, we came across a disciple of Nicodemus that I met last year. We started talking about the kingdom, and he invited us to his house. We baptized two dozen people there, and gained a disciple who wants to follow Jesus closely."

Andrew said, "From there John and I went to Bethlehem, stopping at small villages along the way and proclaiming Jesus. When we got to Bethlehem, I met a man whose father was a shepherd. This shepherd was with a group that saw a band of angels proclaiming the birth of the Messiah. They went to Bethlehem and saw baby Jesus lying in a stable.

"We told him about the kingdom and what Jesus was proclaiming now, and he wanted to be baptized immediately.

Then the rest of his family and a few more in the town became believers also."

Judas of Kerioth said, "Simon and I found the village of Bayt Letepha, in the area we heard was plotting to fight the Romans. Many men there are members of the Zealot party. We proclaimed the good news of the kingdom of God, but they wanted a general who would lead them into battle right away. I told them we had to wait for the Messiah to lead us.

"But when I told them Jesus commanded us to do good things for those who hate us and to pray for our enemies, they wanted to stone us. Then when Simon said our enemies would come from our own households, they started picking up stones. We left that town and shook the dust off our feet against them."

Former Zealot Simon said, "We went from there to the town of Judah and declared, 'The kingdom of God is at hand!' The people there believed our message and wanted to know more. We spent three weeks teaching the good news of Jesus of Nazareth, and many were baptized. They asked us to return after the festival so they can hear more."

Matthew son of Alpheus said, "Before I gave my ink and parchments to Gemariah, I wrote down the instructions that Jesus gave us for our journey. Now that I've heard your stories, I can say that the twelve of us have fulfilled all the instructions he gave us. I'm looking forward to our next month on the road, and reporting back to Jesus all that has happened with us."

Simon son of Alpheus said, "It seems clear that God has been with us."

Epilogue

· ·

Dance of Death

WEDNESDAY 5 JANUARY AD 29, 7:00 PM

"Mother, I'm nervous."

"Salomé, you'll be fine. You've been practicing this dance for months," said Herodias.

"I know, but there's a hundred men out there in the king's court."

"Yes, and when you finish your dance, there will be a hundred men who want to marry you. But you're a princess, and you want to attract a man who will make you a queen. Right now there's four kings out there, and at least a dozen princes who could be kings some day. This is the biggest feast my husband Antipas has ever thrown. It just so happened that his birthday fell on the same day as the Festival of Lights, so everyone's in a party mood. And right here at Fort Machaerus is the best palace to throw a party this side of Egypt."

"Yes, I remember the Festival of Lights last year at Jerusalem. I hope God is with me."

"God? Which god? There's dozens of gods, girl. Pick your own god, Salomé. Just pick one that will help you become a queen like me. That is your destiny. You're the daughter of a queen, and you need to find your king while you're still young and beautiful."

"But you're still beautiful, Mother."

"Huh. Thanks, but that's only because my maids and hairdressers and beauticians and dressmakers worked me over for three hours this morning. I need to keep up appearances if I'm going to keep my throne secure."

"Why? Isn't your throne with Antipas secure?"

"Yes, but that evil man John the Baptist wants to throw me down out of it. He tells my husband, 'It is not lawful for you to have her.' I'd like to go down into the dungeon and gouge his eyes out, but your stepfather won't let me. He's afraid of the people, because they think the Baptist is a prophet. But I'll get rid of him some day, just you watch. You just concentrate on making those men out there want you."

"Do you have any tips on how to do my dance?"

"Don't show too much skin. Keep the mystery alive, and every man out there will be wanting to undress you."

"Oh, don't worry about that, mother. I'm using seven veils, and those men will think they're seeing me naked but it will all be in their imagination."

"Good. None of them is going to forget you. When one of them becomes a king, you can make your move and they'll be sure to remember you."

"Oh, I hear my music starting! It's time for me to go out, when they darken the torches."

"Don't break a leg, sweetie."

"Whoa, I'm out of breath!"

"You were magnificent, Salomé. I was watching from behind the door-curtain. There's a hundred men out there now full of nothing but pure lust."

"Yes, I was watching them. Every table is stacked high with wonderful food, but not one person took a single bite, not even a sip of wine. They were all too busy watching me."

"Wait, here comes an attendant. Are you ready if they want an encore?"

"Yes, I have a second dance prepared."

The attendant came out of the court and approached Herodias. He bowed and said, "Your majesty, the king requests the presence of your daughter in the court. He wishes to speak to her."

"She has my leave to enter," said Herodias.

Salomé followed the attendant into the middle of the room and stood before her father-in-law Herod Antipas. He said to her, "Your dance has pleased the king and his court. We wish to give you a gift in appreciation. Ask me for whatever you wish, and I will give it to you. As God is my witness, whatever you ask of me I will give you, up to half of my kingdom."

"Oh! Thank you, your majesty." She paused and said, "May I have leave to consult my advisor?"

"Yes," he said. "But don't delay long, for the sake of my guests."

Salomé went out and said to her mother, "What should I ask for? If I had half his kingdom I could be queen of Perea, or queen of Galilee. Then you would be queen of the other half."

"Trust me daughter, you don't want that. The Jewish people are troublesome and rebellious, and you would need a strong king at your side before taking that on."

"But what should I ask for?"

"What you want most of all is to make your future throne secure, and that can only be if my throne is also secure. Tell him to give me the head of John the Baptist here on a platter."

Salomé had a shocked look on her face. But she hurried back to the king and said, "I want you to give me at once the head of John the Baptist on a platter."

Now it was the king with a shocked look on his face. He had sworn to the girl to give her what she asked, and his guests would despise him if he broke his oath.

"It will be done," said the king. "Guard, send an executioner with orders to bring me the head of John the Baptist."

Salomé came to her mother carrying the platter with the Baptist's head.[90]

Herodias laughed in triumph. She said, "Victory! Didn't I tell you I'd get rid of him some day? Now it's time to finish the job. I want the heads of all the disciples of John the Baptist, beginning with his most famous disciple. I always get what I want!"

And she said, "What I want on a platter is the head of Jesus of Nazareth!"[91]

Notes and Suggested Bible Readings

1. Matthew 12:1
2. Leviticus 19:9–10; 23:22
3. 1 Samuel 21:1–6
4. Luke 6:1–5
5. Acts of charity called for by the law of Moses. Every person who was able was expected to do good in some way.
6. Matthew 6:1–4
7. John 5:1–9, 13b
8. 2 Samuel 5:6–9, 2 Samuel chapter 9
9. Mark 7:9
10. John 5:10–15
11. Psalm 134
12. Around AD 30, Jewish authorities effectively ruled out the death penalty for those caught in adultery.
13. John 8:2–11
14. John 5:17–29
15. Mark 3:6
16. Matthew 12:9–14, Mark 3:1–6, Luke 6:6–11
17. Matthew 12:14–15a
18. Mark 3:7b–8
19. Luke 8:2–3
20. Mark 3:7–12, Luke 6:17–19
21. Luke 6:12–16, Mark 3:13–19, Matthew 10:2–4, John 1:47
22. Luke 6:20–36, Matthew 5:1–12, 38–48
23. Luke 6:46–49, 13:23–24, Matthew 7:24–28, 13–14
24. Matthew 12:15–21
25. Micah 5:2
26. Luke 7:2–10
27. Joshua 5:13–15

28. Inspired from words used by Pastor Kurt Reeder during a house cleansing in AD 2014.
29. Luke 8:1–3
30. Pentecost
31. Luke 7:11–18
32. *Cf.* Isaiah 57:13,15,16a
33. Matthew 11:20–30, *cf.* ESV
34. Isaiah 35:5; 61:1
35. Malachi 3:1
36. Matthew 11:2–19, Luke 7:18–35 ESV
37. Matthew 11:12 is a reference to Micah 2:13, retranslated with reference to the New Testament in Hebrew. See David Bivin and Roy Blizzard Jr., *Understanding the Difficult Words of Jesus: New insights from a Hebraic Perspective*. Revised edition. Shippensburg, Pa: Destiny Image Publishers, pages 84–87, 2004.
38. Genesis
39. Revelation 16:13–16
40. 1 Maccabees 2:33–41
41. Josephus *Antiquities* 6:272–277
42. Luke 7:36–50 ESV
43. 1 Samuel 28:8–19
44. Matthew 9:28–34; 12:22–32, 43–45, Mark 3:22–29, Luke 11:14–26
45. John 10:19–21
46. Cf. Isaiah 42:1–4, Matthew 12:18–21 NIV
47. Jonah 1:17, 3:5–6
48. 1 Kings 10:1
49. Matthew 12:38–42, Luke 11:16, 29–32
50. Matthew 12:46–50, Mark 3:21, 31–35, Luke 8:19–21
51. Matthew 13:1–52, Mark 4:1–34, Luke 8:4–18
52. Matthew 13:10–16, Mark 4:10–12, Luke 8:9–10
53. Isaiah 6:10–11
54. Mark 4:13–20, Luke 8:11–15, Matthew 13:16–23
55. *Cf.* Matthew 13:24–30, 36–43, 47–50 ESV
56. Ezekiel 17:22–24
57. Matthew 13:31–32, Mark 4:30–32, Luke 13:18–19
58. Mark 4:26–29
59. Matthew 13:33, Luke 13:20–21
60. Genesis 32:24–32
61. Mark 2:19
62. *Cf.* Zechariah 8:19–23

63. Genesis 16:11–12; 28:9
64. Proverbs 2:1–5
65. Matthew 13:44–46
66. Mark 4:21–25, Luke 8:16–18, 11:33–36
67. Matthew 13:51–52
68. Amos 5:8–9
69. *Cf.* Amos 5:21–24
70. Revelation 6:1–17; 8:6–12
71. Matthew 10:34–39, Luke 11:23, Matthew 12:30
72. Matthew 8:18–23, Mark 4:35–36, Luke 8:22
73. Matthew 8:24–27, Mark 4:37–41, Luke 8:23–25
74. Matthew 8:28–33, Mark 5:1–16, Luke 8:26–36
75. Matthew 8:34, Mark 5:17–20, Luke 8:37–39
76. Matthew 9:20–22, Mark 5:21, 24–34, Luke 8:40, 42b–48
77. Matthew 9:18–19, 23–26, Mark 5:22–24, 35–43, Luke 8:41–42, 49–56
78. Isaiah 25:6–9
79. Matthew 22:1–14 ESV
80. Matthew 13:53b–58, Mark 6:1–6a
81. Matthew 9:35–38, Mark 6:6b
82. Matthew 10:1,8, Mark 6:7, Luke 9:1–2
83. Matthew 10:5–15, Mark 6:8–11 Luke 9:3–5
84. Matthew 10:16–20
85. Matthew 10:24–31
86. Matthew 10: 32–33, 40–42
87. Arimathea
88. Hanukkah
89. Psalm 23
90. Matthew 14:3–12, Mark 6:17–29
91. Salomé married two different kings in the years shortly following Jesus' crucifixion. Herodias remained with Herod Antipas into his retirement years.

Thank you for taking the time to read *JOHN and the Jesus Boat Episode Two*. I hope it delighted you to read it as much as it delighted me to write it. Episode Two is the second of four parts following the life of John the Apostle through his appearances in the Bible. Here is a sneak preview from *Episode Three–AD 29*.

"What's going on? This must be important."

"I'm afraid so, John," said Daniel. "King Herod killed the Baptist four days ago."

John felt like he'd just been punched in the stomach. He said, "Oh, no! I'm so sorry, guys!"

"Herod chopped off the Prophet's head," said Linus. "We heard about it from the jailer the next day, and he let us come get the body. We buried him just before Sabbath. But that's not all. It gets worse."

"What could be worse?" said John.

"Word on the street is that Herod wants to finish the job by killing all the Baptist's disciples, starting with the most famous one," said Daniel.

"You guys aren't famous," said John. "Who's he talking about?"

"He wants to give his wife a present: the head of Jesus of Nazareth on a platter."

John and the Jesus Boat Episode Three: AD 29 - Elijah's Mountain will be available for your enjoyment online and at bookstores soon. Get it from Amazon Books, in paperback or on Kindle. You can "like" my author page at Facebook/Author Rolin Bruno for the latest schedule. Tell a friend!

www.ingramcontent.com/pod-product-compliance
Lightning Source LLC
Chambersburg PA
CBHW030324080526
44584CB00012B/699